Communicating School Finance

Communicating School Finance

♦

What Every Beginning Principal Needs To Know

Chuck Waggoner, Ph.D.

iUniverse, Inc.
New York Lincoln Shanghai

Communicating School Finance
What Every Beginning Principal Needs To Know

Copyright © 2005 by Charles R. Waggoner

iUniverse books may be ordered through booksellers or by contacting:

iUniverse
2021 Pine Lake Road, Suite 100
Lincoln, NE 68512
www.iuniverse.com
1-800-Authors (1-800-288-4677)

ISBN-13: 978-0-595-36393-3 (pbk)
ISBN-13: 978-0-595-80828-1 (ebk)
ISBN-10: 0-595-36393-8 (pbk)
ISBN-10: 0-595-80828-X (ebk)

Printed in the United States of America

Contents

CHAPTER 1   First Considerations. 1

CHAPTER 2   The Most Important Person 9

CHAPTER 3   Local Property Tax 16

CHAPTER 4   Local Property Taxes Come Together 25

CHAPTER 5   One Straw—One Source. 33

CHAPTER 6   Let's Have Funds, Funds, Funds 39

CHAPTER 7   Toilet Paper Crisis. 49

CHAPTER 8   Building Your School Budget 54

CHAPTER 9   Sundry Other Stuff 61

CHAPTER 10   Final Things 69

NOTES 75

THE MATRIX REVIEW. 77

HELPFUL WEB ADDRESSES 79

Acknowledgements

I'd like to acknowledge my wife Diana for her practical assistance and personal encouragement. She is my life.

To Jason—the bravest person I know and a wizard to boot.

To Zach—an authentic wizard.

1

First Considerations

If I told you that a galaxy group called MS 0735, which is 2.6 billion light-years from earth (one light-year equals about 5.9 trillion miles), has fallen into a black hole over the past 100 million years and is devouring galactic material in it's wake, and furthermore some of this galactic material was violently ejected from the black hole creating two vast cavities 650,000 light-years in diameter around the black hole,[1] you might say as Strother Martin did in his famous line in *Cool Hand Luke*, "What we have here is failure to communicate."

"What are you talking about?" That would be the conventional response of most folk, unless you happened to be well versed in quantum mathematics and astronomy. Understanding something that is unfamiliar can be a very laborious and intimidating undertaking. I have no fundamental understanding of black holes or what trillions of light years away actually mean.

It is possible that you may never have seen or heard of the movie *Cool Hand Luke*. I am a movie buff, so please excuse my referencing some of my favorite movie lines. If you are interested you can rent the movie and view it. Whether or not I will ever be able to comprehend the vastness of space and it's components is most doubtful, but I'll keep reading on the subject and maybe one day it will become clearer.

Admitting our well-recognized ignorance about many topics is nothing at all of which to be ashamed, and is something that we need to readily admit. Acquaintances know all about our ignorant areas anyway.

So it is with school finance and the budgeting process for most beginning principals. Beginning school principals for the most part, are not well acquainted with and conversant in school finance.

Most beginning principals are not coming from the field of mathematics and fewer still have had any training in accounting. The good news is that the construction of budgets and the district financial structure can be fundamentally understood by most anyone with the inclination. This is not "rocket science," but as with all disciplines (pardon the sports analogy), there are levels of the game within every game. The people who play the school finance game at it's highest level in your district will be the district bookkeeper or the district business manager. The guys and gals that are playing the ultimate high stakes school finance game is the legislature of your state. Your responsibility as the building principal will be to build your site-based budget and help to ensure that all the financial transactions involving your building are properly managed.

All would-be principals know that a major key to success is a fundamental understanding of administration and good communications with the various publics of the school and district. The literature is replete with admonitions concerning the need for principals to have excellent communication skills. Search district principal vacancy notices and this is part of what you will find, all dealing with the ability to communicate:

Is a people-person; a visible leader with 'big picture thinking' who has strong communication skills and who can use these skills to relate to and motivate others.

Is a people-person with strong communication skills.

Be a people-person with proven abilities in communications.

Strong interpersonal people skills.

A proven leader with excellent communication skills.

Is a "people-person" with the proven ability to communicate with and relate to a variety of stakeholder groups.

Communicates well with all population segments.

I have even seen one principal vacancy notification from the state of Connecticut requiring that the person selected be *kind*, which in my mind is likely the most important communication skill that anyone can possess.

Being a kind person is a wonderful attribute for any principal to possess, but there are bounds to the niceness. In my graduate principal preparatory classes, I find it extremely difficult to impress upon the students the absolute importance of not recommending for re-employment to the superintendent and school board any marginal beginning teacher. I recommend this rule of thumb, "If the beginning teacher under consideration is not as good or better than 60% of your current staff, then this person will not improve your instructional program." Be "kind" to your students, to whom you owe your first loyalty, rather than being "kind" to the borderline instructor. Let the individual go somewhere else.

All right already. We get it. Any preferred principal is expected to have good communications skills. After all, being a principal means that you are in the people business and if you can't communicate with your various publics, you likely won't be long as a principal. It is amazing to me how anyone in public education at any level can survive very long without at least a minimum perception of what it takes to function as a good communicator, yet I have met some educators who somehow managed to hang on to their teaching positions over the years despite very questionable listening or speaking skills. When teachers retain their classroom positions without good people skills, the fault can be laid directly at the doorstep of the principal, who lacks the fortitude to take responsibility for the poor teaching performance, and fails to communicate those deficiencies to the dysfunctional teacher.

Leonard had been the principal in the same high school for 30 years. His mathematics teacher "Dave" had been on the staff for 25 years. When I first came on board as the superintendent in the district I heard nothing but complaints about Dave and his teaching methods. After observing him on a number of occasions, it was apparent that Dave was rude to his students and unhelpful if they did not understand a mathematics concept that he was trying to convey. I asked Leonard if Dave had been this way since the beginning of his career, and Leonard assured me that he had. In fact, Leonard had recommended to the superintendent and school board some twenty years earlier that Dave not be retained. Leonard's recommendation was not acted upon. The point is, sometimes dysfunctional teachers are not necessarily the fault of the principal. Just be sure and document your recommendations. If you find yourself in the position where your recommendations are being ignored, it might be time for you to consider a change of venue.

Typically, the teachers who aspire to become and do achieve principalships are not rude and abrasive like our mathematics teacher Dave, but have much better people skills and have a tendency to be overly communicative. They are not necessarily good listeners, just good at expounding their ideas. This is particularly true of superintendents who do enjoy pontificating in certain situations sometimes to the point of ad nauseam. Superintendents are like politicos in many regards. The most successful seem to be those that are gifted with "the gab."

This type of individual is able to enter a room of total strangers and within a short period of time meet everyone in the room and tell his or her life story. This is schmoozing at its finest and is considered to be a very important aspect in communicating and networking, particularly by the schmoozer.

There is one item curiously missing from the list of preferred principal qualifications, as seen on vacancy notifications—"the ability to interpret educational and financial data to the board, staff, and community." Typically, this may be seen as the responsibility of the superintendent of schools or the assistant superintendent in charge of finance. Does this mean that beginning principals need not have a good understanding of school finance? Apparently not, as universities devote a semester in the principal preparation program to something typically called 'school finance;' therefore, it must be important.

Members of the principal's school community do expect the principal to "know a little something" about financial issues when asked and to be able to give simple financial explanations. There will be some basics of school finance and budgeting that principals will be asked to address from time to time.

I ask my students in school finance at the very first class session to assess what are the most valuable items for a beginning principal to understand from a list of choices. Inevitably the students will rank "an understanding of school finance" as a number 5 on the Likert Scale, extremely critical, almost without exception. Perhaps they respond this way because they are enrolled in school finance and they believe that this is the expected response, or perhaps they really believe that they will have massive consuming responsibilities in this area.

All of the 20 items in the assessment seem to be more or less "extremely critical" to the novice principal, as the principal correctly understands that she is responsible for everything that goes right or wrong in the building, therefore everything must be critical in the extreme. I think that this anxiety about school finance and budgets is due to the fact that the new principal feels unprepared in this area and realizes the importance of money in the education process. It is only natural, as building budgets are inevitably linked to the entire education process and when budgets get tight, the entire climate of the district becomes problematic.

ASSESSMENT OF PROSPECTIVE PRINCIPAL'S CRITICAL KNOWLEDGE SURVEY

DIRECTIONS: For the skill items listed, please assess how important you believe each item is for a beginning principal to understand in order to be successful. Use the following scale when making your assessment.

5 = Extremely Critical
4 = Critical
3 = Somewhat Important
2 = Not Critical
1 = Irrelevant

Item	Rating
1. Facilitating and conducting faculty meetings _____	
2. Understanding of school and district finance _____	

3. Establishing a class schedule for students and staff _____

4. Keeping up-to-date with school law issues _____

5. Managing the office staff _____

6. Relating effectively with school board members _____

7. Supervision of instruction _____

8. Classroom monitoring _____

9. Keeping certain records and accounts _____

10. Relating effectively with the superintendent _____

11. Establishing a positive relationship with staff _____

12. Inventory equipment, books, and supplies _____

13. Supervision of extra-curricular events _____

14. Supervise janitors, cooks, other non-certified staff _____

15. Requisition and dispensation of supplies and equipment _____

16. Counseling parents and students _____

17. Being visible in the community _____

18. Flying the American Flag daily _____

19. Monitoring the building and grounds for liability issues _____

20. Organizing fund raising opportunities _____

Fortunately or unfortunately for the students, I try to burst their bubble of anxiety and alleviate their fears somewhat by informing them that yes, a basic understanding of school finance is important, but it is far from the most important skill for the new principal to possess, as evidenced by the vacancy notifications.

I do not want to downplay the importance of school finance for the principal, or I would be out of a teaching job, but the topic needs to be kept in perspective of the total job responsibilities and performance of the principal.

A building principal will not lose her position because of building finances or budgets, unless, of course, the principal is unethical with the funds and/or stealing money that is under the control of the principal. If being unethical in school financial matters is going to be a problem then the person does not deserve to retain his/her job and may (probably should) go to prison.

It is surprising how many principals cannot handle the pop money or the gate receipts without dipping in. All too often this subject comes up as a matter of a newspaper item, or you hear of it through the grapevine as a principal is "quietly" dismissed. *Education Week* reported that several administrators from the 3,300 student-district in Roslyn, New York embezzled over $11.2 million dollars of the district's money in a two-year period of time. Twenty-six individuals were implicated in the misuse of funds.[2] Quite obviously this involved something much more than vending machine money. It should also be apparent that not all the embezzling thieves in the country are collected in Roslyn, New York. Dishonesty in financial matters among school administrators (and others in business—think Enron) is an all too common occurrence throughout the nation.

A major part of being a principal is being ethical. This brings us to our first Matrix, to which if you cannot ethically measure up, you need to stop reading. Stop reading now because we do not need you in public school administration.

MATRIX # 1—If you cannot be ethical and honest please do not assume the leadership position of principal in the school.

The term 'Maxim' is so time-honored, it seems that 'Matrix,' meaning a mold or pattern, is more hip and up-to-date for the younger principal set. Those of you who saw the movie "The Matrix" starring Keanu Reeves know that the Reeves character was able to "download" information almost instantaneously into his cerebellum, be it expertise in karate or a foreign language. (Therefore, modestly speaking, this little book could be likened to a 'matrix' in that it provides instant wisdom.)

There are lots of tomes available for the beginning principal about getting through the first year on the job. Curiously, given short shrift in most of them is anything about school or building budgets and district finance. In one of the best books that I have found (Brock & Grady)[3] about launching a principalship, communication is found in the index over thirty times, but the school budget and financial responsibilities of the principal are mentioned only one time.

I am proud to admit that I took school finance twice. The first time I was working on my principal's endorsement and as time would tell, I was one year away from my first principalship. I still recollect three things about the course. First, I earned a 'B' as my final grade, the only 'B' that I procured. Secondly, the professor gave us an assignment to drive around our own communities and count the number of chimneys on the houses. The point of this assignment, the professor said, was to make us aware of the way that property was taxed in Massachusetts sometime prior to the American Revolution. It seems that the more chimneys a home had the more wealth was indicated, thus more taxes were assessed to the homeowner to pay for the education of the community's children. I remember that there were 1,452 chimneys (from my class notes) in that particular community at the time.

The third thing that I learned from my school finance class did not occur until I got my first principalship. The number of chimneys in the district did not matter one whit about anything, except perhaps keeping the dwellers warm. However, there were 311 chimneys in my town. Old useless learning sometimes dies a hard death.

My first go-around with school finance at the college level I like to equate to trying to force a butterfly too soon out of the cocoon. The school financial applications that I remembered from my first experience with my college school finance class were not proving to be very helpful.

In all fairness to the professor and the institution, I'm sure that I was thoroughly exposed to the basics of school finance, but it did not leave much of an impression. In my second year as a principal I took the school finance class again and this time earned an 'A' and more importantly, actually found some practical application to my administrative duties. When I assumed my first superintendency one year later, financial application in all of its manifestations "came home to roost."

The terms 'Fund—Function—Object' began to have meaning for me. Revenue and expenditures, assets and liabilities, and activity funds all fell into place, because I was actually experiencing the true operational experience of budget management. As a teacher, I never understood why the bookkeeper of the district struggled at her desk long after school was out trying to account for three misplaced cents. Why couldn't she or the principal just give the district the three-cents and everyone go home to supper?

It means so much more when information can become practical and hands-on. Somewhere along the line, we as educators need to come to that realization. The theoretical may be of value, but the total practical immersion into a topic such as school finance is the only practical way to really understand it. There is something to be said for OJT (On the Job Training). I have been a longtime advocate of a paid internship year for principals with the internship being served in more than one building working with different principals.

So then, what does an understanding of school finance really contribute to the competency of the principalship? In the great scheme of things, the principal could expect to focus approximately three percent of his total work year on school budgets and finance. This three percent estimation is based on a 220-day work year, at the ridiculously low number of eight hours per workday. Out of the 1,760 hours available, I would surmise that about 53 hours, or three percent of the principal's time would reasonably be spent on finance. Even though this may be seen as a small amount of time, played out in 'fits and spurts,' as it typically is, it is crucial that the financial tasks be done correctly.

Also, a principal who has any ambitions whatsoever of ever assuming a superintendency puts herself in a better position to assume that role if she has the basic understandings of budgeting and finance.

Being able to communicate the basics of school finance is what this book is all about. Actually, it is about more than communicating finance; it is about the principal being able to carry on an intelligent dialogue about finance and being able to ask the right questions of the people who will know the answer to the financial query.

MATRIX # 2—If you don't know the answer—find someone who does.

This person may be a colleague or another administrator in your district, but the only sure bet is the district bookkeeper or the business manager if your district is fortunate enough to have one. Other than the superintendent, the bookkeeper (and/or business manager) is the one person who actually sees 'the big picture' and has access to all of the information. Do not count on the superintendent if she is just beginning in the position and this is her first superintendency. Particularly in small school districts a new superintendent may be almost as lost in the woods financially speaking as you are.

2

The Most Important Person

My experience with teachers is that when it comes to financial matters of the school district, most do not have a clue and do not care much, as long as their checks show up bi-monthly, some pay raise is provided annually, and the fundamental material necessities of the classroom are provided. This is understandable, as teachers are instructionally busy people and have enough on their plates with No Child Left Behind (NCLB). When the time does come in a career where the teacher is contemplating going into school administration, that would be the appropriate moment to involve oneself in the financial matters of the district.

When contemplating a career change from teacher to administrator is the time to introduce yourself to the district bookkeeper in a meaningful financial way. Having established this relationship will make it much easier when trying to understand the school finance class that you will eventually take. Or, should the teacher never pursue an administration position, at the very least she will become more knowledgeable as a taxpayer and member of the school community about where the money comes from, where it goes, and how it gets reported.

I insist that my school finance students procure a copy of the financial coding of the state in which they find themselves; a copy of the district budget for the current fiscal year; and a current report of the bills paid for the month. Most teachers have never attended a meeting of the board of education, let alone seen a listing of the bills or a copy of the budget. One individual in my class was shocked to find out from the budget that the principal of her building was making in excess of $100,000 per year, not including benefits. My student mentally kicked herself over and over as to why it took her so long to begin the process of administrative certification so that she could be privy to the big bucks.

I have found that teachers who serve on contract negotiation teams often become quite knowledgeable in some aspects of school finance and the budget process, but not many teachers want that particular responsibility or hassle.

The new principal should ask the bookkeeper for the district budget, both the revenue and the expenditure portions, for the past year and the coming year, assuming the school board has passed the new budget. By the time you arrive in your first principalship sometime in the summer, there should be at least a tentative budget available in the central office. If the tentative budget is not available, find out when it might be ready for viewing. Eventually, a budget both tentative and final will be available for you. All states have timelines as to when budgets must be approved by the board of education.

Typically, school districts are set up on fiscal year budgets beginning July 1 and ending on June 30 of the next year when theoretically the books are closed. The concept of 'fiscal year' is easy to understand, but typically not explained very well in textbooks. The assumption is that everyone knows what it means. I have not found that to be necessarily the case.

The federal government and certain other public bodies may conduct their operations based on different fiscal year calendars. (Very few things in life are simple.)

The fiscal year is the period used as the fiscal accounting period. The fiscal year always is one year beyond the beginning of the current school year's budget. For example, if the school year is 2005–2006, the fiscal year budget is FY06. The budget for fiscal year 2006–2007 will be the budget year FY07. It's not hard to understand once you get the hang of it, but can be confusing if you are talking about the FY07 budget and the date is August 20, 2006.

MATRIX # 3: Do not assume anything as a principal when you are communicating financial matters of the building or district. Thoroughly explain your terms; not everyone in your audience has a working understanding.

If the new fiscal year budget is not available yet, try to obtain the tentative one if it has been placed on file prior to school board approval. If you can't get the tentative one, so be it, but at the very least get a copy of the past fiscal year's budget so that you might be able to make some comparisons between fiscal years when the new budget is finalized. It is unlikely as a beginning principal, assuming your duties in August that you will be required to provide much more than cursory input on your building budget.

To project your building's budget, you need to have an understanding of your school's funds and be able to examine the past revenue and spending patterns. In Chapter 6 you will discover that 'funds' are the places where revenue is specifically placed by the rules of the state financial accounting code. The spending patterns are nothing more than how your building spent the money that it was allocated over the past fiscal year.

Your building's money will come primarily from three sources: 1) the school district's operating budget; 2) grants from organizations and the state or federal government; and 3) your students, your parents, your staff, and patrons of the community and other communities.

The school board will develop an annual budget each year with enough money to keep the schools running. The district operating budget will set aside money for salaries, the utilities of your building, the needs of your cafeteria, and the maintenance of your building, for example. The principal does not have to worry about the salaries and benefits for her staff because the central office has developed a budget in great detail that addresses those issues. The principal does not need to agonize over whether the electric bill will be paid. All of the basic necessities will be budgeted for the principal by the kind folk in the central office.

Individual schools within a district typically receive and spend some of the school district's operating budget by category. The superintendent and school board may allow Brown Elementary School $25,000 for textbooks for FY06. This means that the principal is allocated this amount to use for this specific purpose and the $25,000 will be placed in an individual numbered account for the object of textbook purchase.

Principals should be aware that money left unspent in accounts such as textbooks, will go back to the central office at the end of the fiscal year.

Money that is allocated to individual schools by the central office is for such accounts as textbooks, classroom supplies, copy paper, copy machine service contracts, attendance incentive programs, and other esoteric school accounts applicable to specific districts and buildings.

Spending all of the money that the principal is allocated is considered to be wise management, as it is uncertain whether the money returned to the unit office will show up again in the next fiscal year allocations. On the other hand, there are principals that relish in the idea of keeping a tight rein on the purse strings and demonstrating to the superintendent and board how much money they were able to conserve by returning some. Pick your own philosophy of spending your allocations based on what is best for the kids in your building. I say if there is a demonstrated need that the money will improve the education of the kids, then the money needs to be spent.

Another revenue source for your building will be grant funds. Grant funds typically require the principal (or her designee) to file an application with the granting agency. Usually grant dollars are categorical, meaning the use of the money is restricted to a specific educational activity, such as staff development. Grant money must be spent in the fiscal year in which it is received.

The third revenue source for the building will come from money collected from parents, students, and patrons of the communities that your building serves.

Money that you collect from admissions to a volleyball game likely will go into a volleyball fund. Money that students bring to aid in the cost of a field trip will be placed in a field trip account.

Field trip money is an example of a student account. Student accounts contain money raised by the students to be used by the specific student group that raised the funds or the student body as a whole. Another typical example would be the junior class activity fund money which would be used to pay for the junior-senior prom. Activity fund accounts of this type are not spent at the discretion of the principal or sponsor, but should be used only for a stated purpose based on a determination of the students involved. In this sense the money is restricted.

Being a new administrator or a newly financially concerned teacher with administrative ambitions is the time to ask questions of the bookkeeper. No question can be too stupid or embarrassing at this juncture. If you wait until you have been principal for a few months to ask, "What fiscal year are we in?" you might make eyebrows go up and get a snicker. (Not the candy bar.)

Because education is a function of the fifty states, budget forms will likely be different in each state. The good news is that if you are district hopping within a particular state the budget forms of all districts within the state "should" look the same for reporting purposes to the capital city. This enables states to compare districts within the state border to know how much money is being wasted on administration in the various districts. (Just joking, as this is only one of the many purposes of budget reporting.)

The FY district budget will tell you how much revenue is anticipated and from what sources. Depending on the state in which you practice, the revenue source percentages will vary, but fundamentally come only from state, local, or federal sources.

The majority of school funding comes from local and state tax collections, with a lesser amount coming from federal sources. The amount of federal dollars received in a school district depends on the state and the particular school district. Assuming that the principal reports the necessary information to the federal government in terms of child counting, the principal has no control over federal dollars available.

The preponderance of the revenue that is provided to the local district comes from a combination of state and local community taxes. This amount of the split between the state aid dollars and the local community generated dollars varies widely from state-to-state and to some extent within the states themselves. Some of the states have very low property taxes and higher state income taxes. Others have just the reverse.

In addition, within the various states there is a wide range in the taxable value placed upon property. The difference in the total property value from one district to another is often quite extensive and staggering. Everyone understands that the same home in community 'A' is worth more than an identical home in community 'B'. Location, location, location.

MATRIX # 4: It takes money to run the schools and the money will come from only a limited number of sources. No matter the source, you will only be able to utilize the dollar amounts that are available in the budget.

This seems like a simple statement, but try explaining this to the staff when the copy paper budget has been exhausted in April and there are no more dollars left to procure copy paper. (A prudent principal will shift budget amounts around so that the paper keeps flowing.)

Unfortunately, a teacher's budget at home and the school or district budgets are quite different matters entirely. This difference makes it difficult for many teachers to understand, but as a financially communicating principal, you have to make every effort to explain it so that they will fully appreciate the school's economic plight.

The typical teacher's income is generated by her paycheck. From this paycheck the teacher pays the rent or mortgage, the utilities, the car payments, food, medical, entertainment, and so on and so on. The prudent teacher may have established a budget, but when an emergency car repair bill comes along, if there is no money budgeted for car repairs, then the individual will repair the car with dollars that were originally targeted for something else, go without a car, or drive an improperly functioning car, which will only lead to more car expenses down the road.

If the car repairs will require $500, then the teacher must find the $500 somewhere in her budget, tap a savings account, or borrow the necessary money. Typically, if a person looks really hard enough there is some contingency or "fluff" in the individual budget where the money may be taken. Some of life's extras may well have to be eliminated in the coming months to pay for the necessary car repairs when the end of the month comes around.

Yes, I know. The most likely scenario is that the teacher will pay for the repairs with a credit card. School districts do not have the credit card option for paying of bills of this sort, although I have heard of a few administrators that got into problems because of misuse of the district credit card. (Read *MATRIX # 1*.)

A school district conducts its financial affairs in a similar manner as the individual with one important exception. The individual likely has only one source of income, her paycheck. A school district has three main sources of income; state, local, and federal and often the dollars cannot be combined.

The individual teacher has one checkbook, which is the source of the payments of all of her life's expenditures. Even if the prudent person has constructed an individual budget, the money is still paid from "the" checkbook. This is single-entry accounting, sometimes referred to as the checkbook method of accounting.

You record the money you receive in the credit portion of the checkbook and make the payment in the debit column, and write the check to whomever. The money has one home (the balance of the checkbook), but many destinations.

The school district uses a double-entry accounting method of bookkeeping. Under the *Generally Accepted Accounting Principles (GAAP)*, which most states have adopted, school districts must use the double entry form of accounting. This replaced the single entry method or checkbook method.

Governmental bodies, and school districts are governmental bodies, divide their financial operating structures into separate entities known as funds, or accounting funds. A fund is an operating unit that has its own accounting, budgeting system, and set of financial reports. The *GAAP* has been developed by the Governmental Accounting Standards Board (GASB, 2001), which creates the framework of funds for the financial operations of a school district. Fortunately, the principal does not need to know any of this information in any detail, except for understanding that the school accounts are organized by "funds." We will talk about various "funds" later.

The double entry method uses a formula that requires all transactions to have a minimum of two entries in the accounting process. This method also requires that all entries be processed through a system of journals, ledgers, and reports that serve as a check on all transactions that the district makes. The efficient recordings and processing of the transactions lead to the creation of financial reports by the bookkeeper that are reported to the superintendent and school board monthly. From these various reports the administration and school board can track the ebb and flow of funds in and out of the district.

When an individual writes a check for the rent or mortgage payment the checkbook balance is decreased by that amount. This is single entry bookkeeping.

When the school bookkeeper issues a check for dry erase markers, that check will be taken from the school instructional materials, classroom supplies, or some such named line item, which exists as a budgeted item for the fiscal year. The budgeted amount will then be debited.

In the k-12 school business, most of the dollars spent go for salaries and benefits of the people who work for the district.

As principal, you should be privy to the monthly financial reports of the district and your building, but if you don't receive a copy, ask for one. As a principal in a district with multiple buildings, you will have building-wide accounts for which you will be responsible that document financial transactions during most months of the school year. It is absolutely essential that you receive a copy of these reports.

As a new principal it is important to know where the revenue comes from. Why? That's a good question. Having this knowledge is not going to enhance or diminish your revenue in any way, but it will give you a handle on the financial situation of your particular state and district.

You now know that your money comes from the central office, grants that application has been made for, and activity dollars that come from everywhere; bake sales, admission tickets, the school store, etc.

3

Local Property Tax

With the exception of only a couple of states, anyone who owns property receives a property tax billing. It is amazing to me that many people do not understand how this property tax billing is determined.

Property, defined as *Real Property* is not readily movable. This includes land, buildings, and improvements.

The property tax was the first kind of school tax, and still constitutes a very sizeable source of revenue for schools in most states.

Property taxes are expressed in mills per dollar of assessed valuation or in dollars per hundred dollars of assessed valuation. We will look at examples of how to calculate both mills and dollars of assessed valuation, as the states vary on the method used. Find out how your state determines property value for billing purposes. Mills or dollars, it will be consistent throughout a particular school district and state.

For the sake of illustration, let's say that your property consists of a residential family dwelling. There is a person in your community, typically elected, known as the assessor, who determines the value of all property, including yours, for taxing purposes.

How does the assessor arrive at a dollar value for your property? If you recently purchased your property for $200,000 then this amount is on record in the courthouse. Property that was purchased for $200,000 then is valued at $200,000.

If you have lived in your house for a number of years and property in the community similar to yours has recently sold, then the assessor may determine your property's value in this manner. Property increases in value over time. If you purchased your home thirty-years ago, have maintained it rigorously, and the neighborhood has not remarkably deteriorated, then your home is worth more now than it was thirty years ago. It is likely that your tax bill has kept up with the added value of your home being increased each year, but likely not nearly as much as if you were to purchase your home today. When a similar home to yours sells on your street or neighborhood, you might expect to see a more dramatic tax increase than normal. Fair is fair.

Unfortunately, property tax is not a particularly fair way to fund schools. There is widespread unfairness in property assessment in many states and localities. The scope of this brief book is not to necessarily argue the merits or failures of the property tax. It seems elemental to say that public education will have to be funded by the public in some manner, be it by property taxes, sales taxes, income taxes, so-called sin taxes, luxury taxes, riverboat and casino taxes, taxes on services, taxes on personal property, or some other of the many creative ways that we are taxed by our elected officials.

The legislature of Texas spent most of the summer of 2005 trying to agree to a tax-swap funding bill that would more adequately pay for education in that state. Governor Perry was quoted in the *Dallas Morning News* on July 21, 2005 as saying "Education reform and property tax relief are the two most significant issues the legislature faces." As an aside, I wonder if education reform and property tax relief are even compatible terms.

Reliance upon the property tax for funding education has been a forever-ongoing battle in several states. For the new principal, this funding source is a reality of life.

It would be good if you, as the principal, have an understanding of your own tax billings and how to calculate the expected revenue of the school district based on the assessed valuation of all of the taxable property in the district. It is likely that a stakeholder in the district might ask for an explanation of the property taxing process someday, particularly when tax increases are contemplated. Everyone wants to know how much more they will pay in property taxes. Not having to bother the superintendent or bookkeeper with a question that you can answer is typically an adroit opportunity to impress someone.

Your property tax bill will arrive sometime in the early summer to early fall from the county treasurer. The bill will contain a legal description of the property including the location. The property will be assessed in two ways, the value of the land itself and the value of any improvements to the land, which typically are the home and/or other structures. There is a full-value placed on the land and the property. This might be better thought of as "fair market value," what you would receive for your property if it were sold on the open market.

There is also a taxable market value that is placed on the property for taxation purposes. This is where it becomes mildly confusing until you have been through the process a time or two.

Property owners do not pay taxes on the total value of their property. They pay property taxes based on the "equalized assessed value." The assessed value is a percentage of the total property value.

For example, this is what the taxes allocated portion of the tax bill might look like for a homeowner whose property was valued at $69,891.

Example 1:

Value-Type	Full-Value	Taxable Value
Land	$3,825	$1,275
Improvements	$66,066	$22,022
Total	$69,891	$23,297

The owner will be presented a tax bill based on the 'equalized assessed value' (EAV) of his property at a figure of $23,297. As you will notice from the example, $23,297 (the amount of dollars on which the taxes will be paid) is one-third of the $69,891, which represents the total value placed on the property. Therefore, we can say that property is assessed at 33.3333% or one-third of the fair-market value in this particular state. States assessing at one-third of the fair-market value is typical, although different percentages may be used by various states. The good news is that whatever percentage is used to calculate the bill will be consistent within each individual state. If you live in New Mexico and your property is assessed at one-third fair market value, all property in the state of New Mexico will be so assessed.

Nowhere on any property tax billing that I have ever seen will it tell the property owner what percentage the taxable amount is based on. This is a percentage that the property owner will have to calculate from the bill, simply by dividing the taxable amount by the total value amount. ($23,297 divided by $69,891 gives you thirty-three and one-third percent infinitum.)

The total value of all of the property in the school district is the value of all the land, buildings, and improvements of the residential, industrial, agricultural, commercial, or unused (vacant land) that can be found and is taxable in the district. Keep in mind that some property is not taxed, such as religious, state or federally owned property.

In our example, the $69,891 valued home would be considered modest in many communities. Let's take a look at a hypothetical tax bill for a large productive farm and improvements (home) of considerable worth.

Example 2:

Value-Type	Full-Value	Taxable-Value
Land	$750,000	$247,500
Improvements	$200,000	$66,000
Total	$950,000	$313,500

Once again we see that the taxable-value is based on thirty-three and one-third percent of the full-assessed value of the property. There is a considerable amount of difference that the owner of a $69,891 property is going to pay in local property tax compared to the individual that owns the $950,000 property, even when both are reduced to the equalized assessed value.

It should be obvious why large property owners are very reluctant to pass school district requests for property tax increases. The owner of the more valuable property feels as though he is subsidizing the education of the children coming from the property worth $69,891. It sometimes makes it exponentially more difficult to convince those paying large property tax bills to increase the amount when they have no children or grandchildren attending school in the school district.

Our next step is to determine exactly what the tax-amount will be for our two properties.

On the tax bill the property owner will find a line detailing the tax-rate and the tax amount. It may very well look like this from our $23,297 first example:

Total	Tax-Rate	Tax-Amount
$23,297	9.102	$212.05

From the second example of the more extensive farm and residence that had a total fair-market value of $950,000, the line will appear as:

Total	Tax-Rate	Tax-Amount
$313,500	9.102	$2,853.48

There is an obvious difference between a tax bill of $212.05 and one of $2,853.48. It is true that the person paying the higher property tax is theoretically and in all practicality much better financially healed, but that does not make paying the tax any more pleasant for them. Typically, affluent folk can be very tightfisted with their money.

At this point, you should be asking the question "What is the Tax-rate of '9.102' all about?" That is a fair question. Let me try to explain. The state where this tax bill was presented bases its tax rates on something called "a mill". A mill is equal to $.001 or one-tenth of a cent. 100 mills equal 10 cents and 1000 mills equate to one-dollar.

Look at Example 1 again. The taxable amount was $23,297 and the tax rate was 9.102. Somewhere on the tax bill it should be noted that the tax rate is expressed in mills, but this may not be the case. (The tax rate may be expressed in dollars, as we will see later.) A homeowner may have to call the county treasurer to find out how the tax rate is expressed. At any rate, we now know that one-mill equals .001 of a cent and that there are 1000 mills in a dollar.

The taxable amount of $23,297 is divided by 1000 because the tax rate is expressed as 9.102 mills and there are 1000 mills in a dollar. $23,297 divided by 1000 which is taken times the tax rate of 9.102 = $212.05 (rounded). Try it. It works.

Let's see if we can calculate the property tax in mills of Example 2. In this example the value of the land and improvements were equalized (33 1/3% of the total value) as $313,500. We know that the tax rate expressed in mills is 9.102. We divide $313,500 by 1000 (because there are 1000 mills in a one-dollar) and we get 313.5 mills. The 313.5 is multiplied by the tax rate of 9.102 mills for a final tax billing of $2,853.48 (rounded off by my cheap calculator.) With your calculator you should get a similar figure. A penny or two one way or the other likely reflects the rounding peccadillo of one of our devices.

As I mentioned earlier, your state may equalize property values, which is referred to EPV (*Equalized Property Value*) or sometimes as EAV *(Equalized Accessed Valuation)* by multiplying the total value of the property by a percentage figure. In the examples we have used so far that figure has been 33 1/3% of fair market value. To review, a property assessed at $333,333 fair market value has an equalized property value (EPV) for taxing purposes of $111,111. This is calculated by multiplying $333,333 times 33 1/3%. Multiplying by 33 1/3% gets hairy on cheap calculators like mine, I think because they are not "big" enough, but you should arrive at a dollar amount of something close to $111,111. Have no fear; the people in the courthouse sending out the tax bills do have calculators that are up to the task.

It is easier to accurately calculate if your state uses a rounded percentage to equalize the property value such as 20% of fair market value to calculate the bills.

Many states will use the 20% figure. If this is the case your tax billing sttement will look like this:

Example 3:

Value-Type	Full-Value	Taxable Value
Land	$6,000	$1,200
Improvements	$159,000	$31,800
Total	$165,000	$33,000

In this example the full-value of the property was multiplied by 20%, which is the figure that this state uses to arrive at the equalized assessed value. Assuming now that the tax rate is expressed in mills and that the rate is the same as we have been using, 9.102 mills, what is the taxable amount on the property in Example 3?

Remember that 1000 mills equal $1.00. We must divide the total EPV or EAV of the property ($33,000) by 1000, for a calculation of 33. The 33 is multiplied by the tax rate of 9.102 mills for a tax bill of $300.37.

In Example 3 the EPV was based on 20% of fair-market value. What would you expect if the EPV was based on 33 1/3% of fair-market value as was used in our previous examples? Would the property owner being paying more or less property taxes? You may calculate it out for yourself, but logic would dictate that if you pay on 33 1/3% of something you would expect to make a bigger payment that if you paid on 20% of something.

Let's try a couple of review problems. (1) If the taxable value of your property is established as $30,000 (remember that the taxable value is the EAV or EPV) and the tax rate is .93 mills, what is your tax billing?

How about one more problem with an additional step? (2) The fair-market value of your property is $100,000 and the state bases the EAV or EPV at 20% of fair-market price. What is your tax bill if the tax rate is 1.17 mills?

The answer to (1) is $30,000 divided by 1000 (1000 mills in $1) and take the answer times .93 mills. The answer is a tax billing of $27.90. The answer to (2) is slightly more complex because you must first find out what 20% of $100,000 is. I'm betting you can see that the answer is $20,000 even without the benefit of a calculator. Now, divide the $20,000 by 1000 (1000 mills in $1) and take the answer, which is 20 times the tax rate of 1.17 mills. The answer is $23.40.

Looking at question (1) again, can you determine what the fair-market value of the property was if the taxable value was $30,000 and the state assessed at

20%? Of course you can. The answer must be a number that $30,000 is 20% of. How do we find out what that number is? Simply divide $30,000 by .20 (20%) and you will get $150,000. $150,000 then was the established fair-market value of the property if the property was assessed at 20%.

But what if the $30,000 EAV had been assessed at 33 1/3%? This time you divide the $30,000 by .3333 (33 1/3%) and you will arrive at $90,009 or something very close depending on your individual calculator. Make sense?

We have been working with mills because several states calculate property tax rates in that manner, but not all states. Some states, such as Illinois, construct the tax rates using dollars and cents. The principle is just the same as it is with mills only you must be aware if the rate is established in mills or dollars. It makes all the difference in the world in figuring out the tax bill.

Let's use the same figures that we did in Example 2, only this time we will calculate the tax rate in dollars and cents. Remember Example 2 looked like this:

Value-Type	Full-Value	Taxable-Value
Land	$750,000	$247,500
Improvements	$200,000	$66,000
Total	$950,000	$313,500

The taxable-value is still based on thirty-three and one-third percent of the full-assessed value of the property. This time, however, the tax rate will be the same 9.102 but it will be calculated at $9.102 instead of 9.102 mills.

To review the calculation of the mill process: because there are 1000 mills per dollar, we must divide the total taxable value of Example 2, which was $313,500 by 1000, giving us once again 313.5 mills. The 313.5 is multiplied by the tax rate of 9.102 mills, giving us a tax billing of $2,853.48 (plus or minus a cent or two).

Now, if our tax rate is $9.102 we are going to do a similar but somewhat different process and arrive at a much different tax bill.

Everyone knows that there are 100 cents in one dollar; as opposed to the average man in the street knowing that there are 1000 mills in one dollar. We have an EAV of $313,500. This time we divide by 100 because there are indeed 100 cents in a dollar. $313,500 divided by 100 equals $3,135. We multiple the $3,135 by the tax rate of $9.102, because you remember that we actually pay taxes per $100 of EAV, and we get a tax billing of $28,534.77

On the same property, when the tax rate was established as 9.102 mills, the bill was $2,853.48. The tax rate calculated as $9.102 is $28,534.80 (rounded), quite a difference. The astute property owner would, in this case, much rather have his tax bill expressed as mills rather than dollars. The reality is that you have no choice. Your state will either use mills or dollars.

At this point you might be asking yourself, how will I know whether to calculate the tax bill in mills or dollars? That is a very good question and one that deserves some semblance of an adequate answer. I have seen a plethora of property tax billings in my day and I am yet to find a tax bill that says something such as "this was calculated in mills, or this was calculated in dollars." If all else fails, revert back to *MATRIX # 2—If you don't know the answer—find someone who does*. However in this case you may be able to determine the answer yourself as the answer may be a matter of some common sense.

Let's look at the example of my old property tax bill from Illinois circa 2002 and see what makes sense. (Remember that I already told you that Illinois calculates the tax rate in dollars and cents.)

Example 4:

Value-Type	Full-Value	Taxable-Value
Land	$7,500	$1,500
Improvements	$84,000	$16,800
Total	$91,500	$18,300

Can you tell that the EAV or EPV is calculated at 20 percent of fair-market (full-value) on my tax bill? $1,500 is 20% of $7,500. $16,800 is 20% of $84,000. $18,300 is 20% of $91,500. Let's prove the last amount. $91,500 times .20 equals $18,300.

My total tax rate was 9.4174 and my tax bill was $ 1,723.38. The county court house will provide you with your tax billing, and the tax information, but as I said, it will not likely tell you whether or not mills or dollars were used in the calculation. They will just provide you with a total tax rate (in this case) of 9.4174. You will have to call the courthouse and ask mills or dollars, see your bookkeeper or someone else from *MATRIX # 2*, or calculate for yourself, backwards.

Working backwards, you know that my EAV was $18,300 and that the tax rate was 9.417 and my total bill was $1,723.38. The question is, was the bill calculated in mills or dollars? We understand that there are 1000 mills in a dollar. If the 9.417 referenced mills, we would have divided $18,300 by 1000. This equals 18.3, which we take times the rate of 9.417 (assume mills), giving us a billing of

$172.33. This is not my tax bill, which has been established by the county collector/clerk as $1,723.38.

So, let's try the EAV of $18,300 and a tax rate of 9.417 (dollars this time). We divide the $18,300 by 100 (100 cents in a dollar) and we get 183. 183 is taken times the tax rate of 9.417. The bill this time is $1,723.31. This figure matches, or almost matches, my actual tax bill of $1,723.38. (Remember—my calculator, your calculator, and the one that they use in the courthouse—all have different price tags and no doubt round accordingly. We are close. Sometimes you just settle for close.)

MATRIX # 5—If you can't explain something that affects you directly (such as your own tax bill) then the assumption is likely to be that you have some gaps in your understanding of how the district is funded.

Calculating personal tax rates and district expected revenues from local dollars is not a particularly difficult proposition once you see how it is done. Using either mills or dollars is really just a matter of decimal point sliding, but from my experience with prospective principals it is not a topic that is generally well understood.

4

Local Property Taxes Come Together

I read recently that a group of Illinois large-district superintendents have put forth a plan that would transfer much of the dollars for school funding from the property tax to the Illinois state income tax. The plan has been introduced as legislation and has found its way to both the Illinois Senate and House docket. The problem with this brilliant idea is that I know for certain that it has been making the rounds in Illinois since at least 1974 when I first became a school administrator in that state and has been introduced as legislation on several prior occasions. These resolutions are always defeated because to lower property taxes you have to find another funding source, and the only other consistent and logical funding source is increasing state income taxes. Illinois has a relatively low state income tax, which could be raised to help fund schools. (In Texas, state income taxes are illegal per the Texas Constitution.) Most everyone in Illinois pays the state income tax, but only property owners, of course, pay the property tax.

The transfer of public school funding from property taxes to the state income tax made sense in 1974 and it is still completely logical today; however, there is a major stumbling block. The state legislature will not raise taxes, which they would have to do to increase the state income tax. Very few politicos want to seek reelection on the fact that they have increased taxes of their constituents. Their opponents would have a "hay day" exploiting that issue with the electorate and many of those supporters of the state income tax increase would be cast out of the legislature. They can't have that.

Matrix # 6—Politicians have one goal and that is to be re-elected to office. (All right. Maybe there is a politician that is an exception somewhere, so let's preface this Matrix with "99.9999% of all.")

Bush 41 is the perfect example. "Read my lips—no new taxes." He famously reneged on his pledge and the pundits say that this (in no minor part) cost him the presidential election in 1992.

Can you image an Illinois legislator running on the platform—"We increased your income taxes—but notice, you are paying less property taxes. AND YOUR SCHOOLS ARE MUCH BETTER."

If I were the political opponent I would simply say—"Senator Smith increased the Illinois state income tax by 3%. He is a tax increaser and you have fewer dollars in your pocket today because of him and his ilk. That is all I really need to say and harp on, but I could take it a step further and give him some credit for "having allegedly spent the extra dollars to fix Illinois schools, BUT ARE THE SCHOOL SYSTEMS ANY BETTER?" The answer is 'No' to the question are the school systems any better, because inevitably the citizens are going to be disappointed about what happens in the public schools in general. The media will see to this. Research shows that most citizens feel that U.S. schools are not "doing the job."

William J. Banach, a Michigan educator, put it this way in a speech he gave a few years ago:

"Adults should be careful about saying today's young people don't know anything. In a California school district, 120 adults, most with college degrees, were given a 10th grade competency test that measured reading, writing and arithmetic skills. In each of the areas measured, the 10th grader public school students scored higher than the adults.

When we hear about the number of high school graduates who cannot read today, we often forget how many functionally illiterate 60-year-olds are walking around."

Banach concluded: "In America we educate a student for about $7,500 a year. That's barely $7 an hour. And for that $7 we transport kids, feed them, check their ears, eyes and teeth, help them deal with substance abuse, counsel them and educate them. Do you know, you can't go bowling or see a movie or do a whole lot of other things for $7 an hour."[4]

A lot can go wrong in any given school house on any given day that has the potential to upset people. This is not to mention the poor test scores of NCLB, which are caused in no small part because parents have left their child behind for four or five years before they ever enter the public schools, and continue to leave them behind when they come home from school at night, and on the weekends, and during the summer.

Schools may not teach every child exceptionally well in all circumstances, but believe me, from a career that spans almost four decades in education, there are parents that are not parenting very well either. I do not want to make it sound like I blame the educational malaise all on the parents. I do not; however, there is an expression about silk purses and sow's ears that does have some application.

In the excellent book *Freakonomics* the authors discuss the difference between a "good school" and a "bad school."[5] A bad school has certain indicators such as, "gang problems, nonstudents loitering in front of the school, and lack of PTA funding. These schools offer an environment that is simply not conducive to learning."

An "environment not conducive to learning" is typically found where the funds necessary to provide that conducive atmosphere are skimpy at best. This "little or no learning taking place" likely will translate into poor test scores, wouldn't you think?

As this book goes to press, SB750 (Senate Bill) with a companion House Bill is considered as the top priority among schools leaders in Illinois. The essence of SB750 is that the reliance on property taxes to fund the schools of Illinois creates spending iniquities of over $10,000 per student depending on the property wealth of the district in which the child is attending school. This has been termed as "unconscionable" in a letter designed to be sent home to parents to promote the property tax for income tax swap. Illinois has one of the worst funding gaps in the nation between poor and rich school districts. The average funding in Illinois' poorest districts is $4,330 per student while the average funding in the wealthiest districts is $7,249. This translates into a funding gap of 67%, almost three times the national average.[6]

The *Chicago Tribune* reported on August 1, 2005 in a front-page story that the gap between the richest and poorest districts in Illinois grew even wider during the last school year. The difference between the highest and lowest spending districts in Illinois per pupil in the 2003–04 school years was $19,361 per pupil, about $4,000 higher than the preceding year.

The United States Census Bureau data for 2002–2003 shows that the spending per pupil for elementary-secondary education ranges from a high of $13,328 for the District of Columbia to a low of $4,860 for Utah.

Recall that there are three fundamental funding sources for public schools. The dollars are derived from state sources, local sources, and federal sources. (It's all tax dollars of some form or another. Money does not grow on trees you know.)

It is interesting to view how the states compare in terms of the money received per pupil from local sources compared to money from state sources. A comparison of two states shows the fundamental difference in school funding approaches. In Illinois (according to U.S. Census Bureau data for 2002–2003) 62% of the dollars came from local sources and 39% from state coffers. While in New Mexico the figures are fundamentally reversed with 12% of the dollars per pupil from local sources and 86% from state sources.

When I moved to New Mexico from Illinois I purchased a $90,000 home and paid $618 in property tax. In Illinois I had a $60,000 home and paid $1,800 in property tax. However, the flip side of that is that Illinois has a lower state income tax rate than does New Mexico. Once again, the taxpayer will pay for the schools; it is just a matter of how the states break down the revenue sources.

I have no faith that the property tax method of financing education in Illinois or other states where it is the primary educational financial contributor to education will ever be changed. The legislators find it much easier for the local taxpayers to determine for themselves if they want to increase their property taxes to better fund their own local school systems. In most cases the local property owners are not so inclined to raise their taxes, making it very difficult for tax referendums to have any success in Illinois. Illinois is by no means unique in this situation.

I vividly remember when the Lotto came to Illinois. This was to be the way that education was saved, and playing the Illinois Lotto was sold as a "way to contribute to education in Illinois." The plan was that a gigantic chunk of Lotto dollars would go to funding education.

The citizens were told that some Illinois Lotto dollars did find their way to the state education funding formula, but the ensuing political reality was that for every new Lotto dollar, the state legislature requisitioned less of their state income tax dollars to Illinois schools. The result was a wash of funding, leaving the schools no better off than before. The legislature could get more political capital from funding other "more visible" projects for their constituents than increasing school aid.

The over reliance on the property tax (local district wealth) to provide the dollars for education is being played out not in Illinois alone, but in many states across the nation. In the state of Montana, the Montana Supreme Court has ruled that the state's reliance on the property tax to fund public elementary and secondary education in that state violates the Montana Constitution.

In January 2005 the Kansas Supreme Court ruled in *Montoy v. State of Kansas* that the state legislature is violating the Kansas state constitution's requirement that the state must provide adequate funding for public schools. (This is over reliance on local district wealth again.)

The *Associated Press* reported on June 16, 2005 that schools were in danger of not opening in Kansas for the coming school year because the Supreme Court of Kansas will not allow the districts to spend a penny on schools until the legislators fixed the funding system. The Court agreed that Kansas spends too little money on education and distributes it's aid unfairly to districts with poor children, minorities and struggling children.[7]

The North Carolina Supreme Court upheld a trial court's ruling that the state had failed in it's duty under that state's constitution to provide students in the poorest school districts with the "opportunity to attain a sound basic education." The pertinent cases involved are *Leandro v. State,* 488 S.E.2d 249 (1997), and more recently *Hoke County Board of Education v. State of North Carolina* (2004).

Call me pessimistic, but I believe that in Illinois and in other states that rely on the property tax to fund education, administrators are just going to have to live with it. What can the principal of a local school do to mend this problem? The answer is I'm afraid, very little. It is the hands of the legislators and sometimes the Supreme Court of the states to figure school funding out. The poor principal just rides the waves.

Let's take a look at how the reality of local property tax that the individual pays to their school district (that we learned about in Chapter 2) coupled with all the other property tax assessments of the district contributes to the wealth of the school district.

Begin with a comparison of two school districts in Illinois, both of which I am adequately familiar. For our illustration we will have our tax bills be in dollars (as they are in Illinois), but the concept and comparison is easily transferable to a state that taxes in mills, such as Texas and New Mexico. We will transfigure dollars into mills again later for practice purposes.

District 'A' has a total property tax value of $55,000,000. By total property tax value, I mean the total assessment of all property within the boundaries or confines of this particular school district, which we are calling District 'A'.

If I live in District 'A' and my home and land have a fair market value of $150,000, then my $150,000 is a small part of the total district assessment of $55,000,000.

Looking at my $150,000 property assessment, you will remember from Chapter 2, that my property will be assessed on a certain percentage as determined by state legislation. Let's hypothesize that my EAV will be 33 1/3% of the total tax billing, or I will be paying taxes on $49,500. Remember how we arrived at the

EAV? Multiply the tax bill of $150,000 times the determined multiplier, in this case 33 1/3%. On a cheap calculator, like I have, you multiply by .33, which is not 33 1/3%, but close enough for our purposes.

MATRIX # 7—As a principal, sometimes you just have to settle for "close enough" and let it go.

Are we done with my tax bill of $49,500? Do we now take it times the local school tax rate of $4.32? You know better. You remember that the tax bill in Illinois is based on $100 per equalized assessed valuation (EAV). Divide my equalized assessed property worth of $49,500 by $100 and we have a figure of $495. This is the $495 on which my taxes will be paid.

If the school tax rate is $4.12 per $100 of EAV, then to calculate my individual tax bill I take the $495 times the $4.12 tax rate and find that a school tax bill of $2039.40 awaits payment.

The total tax assessment of District 'A' was $55,000,000. The same principle applies. The $55,000,000 fair market value of all the property is multiplied by the multiplier of 33 1/3%, or for us on our calculator, .33. The total EAV then for District 'A' is $18,150,000. The district tax rate of $4.12 per $100 of EAV ($18,150,000 divided by $100 = $181,500 X $4.12) generates $747,770 of local tax dollars for District 'A'. Remember that $2039.40 of the $747,770 comes from my property tax bill.

Is District 'A' a rich district in which to have your kids enrolled or a poor district? Typically, this would be a poor school district. Why? Assume that there are 300 pupils in the district. The wealth per pupil from local dollars is $2,492. This figure is arrived at by dividing the $747,770 of local revenue dollars by 300 pupils. If there were 600 pupils in this school district then the amount per student of local generated dollars is $1,246.

I contend that this district is poor because a child can not be educated for $2,492 per year (assuming a total student population of 300) or certainly not $1,246 if there are 600 students in the district. Even the state with the lowest figure per pupil spending amount (Utah) spends $4,860 per student, per 2002–2003 data. To meet the U.S. average for spending per pupil (2002–03) of $8,019, additional revenues of $5,527 would need to be found (assuming 300 students) or $6,773 (assuming 600 students). This additional revenue takes the form of state aid. Typically, a state will determine what the cost of an adequate education is per pupil and establish that figure as a "foundation level." If the foundation level is set at $8,019 then the dollars necessary to meet this standard for our hypothetical District 'A' would come in the form of state aid, as this district will generate only $1,246 per student with local property tax dollars. The state determines that $8,019 is needed, then an additional $6,773 is necessary in the form of state aid. Quite simply the state takes the 300 students times $6,773 and translates this into $2,031,900 in state aid, bringing District 'A' up to the foundation level.

This is a vast over simplification on my part because most states have factors for state aid based on categories of students (it takes more money to educate a high school student than an elementary student, and more money to educate a special needs student of any ilk). State aid is calculated on a WADA (Weighted Average Daily Attendance). The state will pick a day or two each year when the enrollment of the district is broken down and reported to the state. Typically, the WADA is the basis for state aid entitlements. It becomes much more complicated than this (the school finance game within the game) and if you wish to become an expert become a business manager. This may seem like flippant advice, but as a beginning principal you have enough new stuff on your plate without dipping into the intricate state aid formula.

All of this is beyond the job description of the principal, but remember that you may need to communicate how the game is played to your constituency on some occasion.

To further demonstrate the inadequacy of the local property tax, let's take a look at an urban district with a student enrollment 47,000 students, which we will term 'District B.'. The EAV of this district is $59,220,000. The EAV per pupil is $1,260 ($59,220,000 divided by 47,000). A tax rate of $3.00 of EAV per pupil brings in $37.80 per pupil. How was this figure arrived at?

Remember that the tax rate of $3.00 is based on $100 per EAV. The $1,260 EAV per pupil must be divided by 100 and then taken times the $3.00 tax rate.

Leaving our urban district of 47,000 students behind, let's now take a look at a neighboring suburban district of 3,500 students with an EAV of $98,000,000. This is 'District C'. The EAV per pupil in the suburban district is $28,000 per pupil. If the tax rate is still $3.00 as in the previous example, the suburban district realizes $8,400 per pupil compared to the $37.80 in the urban district. Despite what anyone believes, I think that I can educate a child better with $8,400 per year than $37.80. Most would agree, I trust.

As disparaging as the difference may seem between the urban and suburban districts the example is real. In reality, the families in the suburban district will have a school tax rate considerably higher than the example of $3.00, generating even more local dollars per pupil. It is not uncommon for districts of this type to have more than one swimming pool and many of the 'bells and whistles' of small colleges.

Most discouraging to the folk in Texas is that they have operated under what is termed "The Robin Hood" system. As with the Robin Hood of antiquity, richer schools in Texas must send "excess" locally generated dollars to poorer school districts. In essence, richer school districts in Texas provide dollars in excess of $305,000 (2002–03) per WADA to poorer districts. They do get a choice of which district they would like to receive the extra money, making friends in the process, I am certain.

I can not envision such a concept playing out in Illinois, although this is exactly what happens through the general state aid distribution. Districts just do not know where their excess dollars are going precisely.

5

One Straw—One Source

Max Stirner likened himself to a singer in the heights of his song, who sings for his own sake, not for anyone else, and not for the sake of truth. Beginning principals all too often find themselves like Stirner, caught up in the music of the building financial situation and school budget allocations and not sure what the truth really is.

I have a friend in the principalship that equates his school budget to "that one big sucking straw, which sucks money from the one big source." My friend is correct. Fundamentally, for the school principal there is one source of funds and that source is whatever the central office allocates, based on the total revenue for the district. We now know that the preponderance of your building money will come from the central office through the district collection of tax funds and whatever state aid that the district may receive.

Where does the central office get their money? From three basic sources. Those sources are the federal government, the state government, and from local revenue, generated through the local property tax. Depending on the state that you live in, the percentage from each of the revenue sources differ. There are states that rely heavily on the local property tax and there are states that rely more on the state for their funding. The federal government is a relatively small player in public school funding, averaging about seven percent of total revenue. As with all things, some states get more federal dollars than others, depending on complicated allocated Congressional formulas that are generally not understood, even by Congress.

In my former home state of Illinois there is a joke about school finance. The joke goes something like this—"There are only two people in the state that understand the school aid formula and they are never allowed to be together in one place, just in case the worst should happen." The truth of the matter is that this whimsy can be applied to most states and most school districts. In fact, a school district is lucky if there is one person on board who deeply understands

33

school finance. Fortunately, a total immersion in financial understanding is not really necessary for the principal. Remember, as the principal you are at the mercy of the big pool of money, of which you have no control. Before discouragement sets in let me explain two of the sources of school funding in some detail (remember, there are three sources of district revenue—local, state, and federal).

Federal money we can dispose of quickly. Federal dollars are allocated through grants such as Title I, Title V, the Vocational Education Act, 94–142, bilingual education, and others. Federal money is typically based on a formula per number of children served in the district within a particular category. Although the principal has no control over the amount of federal money allocated, there are monitoring responsibilities of how the money is to be spent and was spent.

If you are lucky enough to have a vocational director, a Title I director, a bilingual education director, etc., to help you track the dollars and fill out the required reports, you are fortunate. If not, revisit *MATRIX # 2—If you don't know the answer, find someone who does.*

In a small school district without the benefit of a program financial specialist, this "someone who does know" will be your bookkeeper. Unless you are dealing with a completely new federal grant, there will be a paper trail of forms from preceding years. This brings us to:

MATRIX # 8—The best predicator of the future is the past. Find out all you can about what has gone before.

This is also known as "future events casting their shadows before them." In the case of following the paper trail of grants, pattern yourself off what has gone before. You have a matrix (pattern) to follow.

As far as the principal is concerned it does not really matter what is the ultimate source of the money. It is sufficient to know that there is a finite pool of money from which your building will draw dollars. If you are dealing with a vocational grant, the paper trail indicates how the money has been spent in the past. For example, if your last year's vocational grant was for $105,000 and $45,000 went to pay the salary and benefits of the instructor, then unless you can find another funding source for the salary, it would be an obvious consideration to continue the practice, keeping in mind salary increases that may have occurred.

What happens if there are suddenly no more grant dollars available? Then you have a problem that will call for creativity on your part and guidance from the superintendent and school board. If the salary can be paid from general funds then the instructor can be retained. If not, then the district may need to consider a reduction in the program.

Sometimes a principal has difficulty communicating what grant funding is all about to school boards, other teachers, and the community. When I began my last new superintendency the district had no early childhood program for students at-risk ages 3 and 4. Having applied to the state for the grant twice before at other districts, I knew that it was a relatively easy process and I believed that it was a very necessary program to help the students be better prepared for kindergarten.

After consulting with the state department of education, it was determined that the district was eligible for $65,000 in early childhood funds. This was certainly enough money to pay for the teacher's salary and benefits, a classroom aide if the number of students went beyond twelve, and all of the necessary supplies to begin the program.

Convincing the board of education was easy. It was a new program that could be justified by the needs of the community, and what's more, it would not cost the district a penny. Unfortunately, over time with the change of board members and the arrival of difficult financial problems for the district, this program became a constant "whipping boy" of several staff and community members. What is this program costing the district? Can't we eliminate it and save the money? The answer is that it is costing the district nothing and if we eliminate the program we abolish a valuable program for no reason.

With the arrival of financial difficulties all programs become suspect and need to be financially justified. The tendency is "wanting to throw someone else's program off the boat" to save money and save another particular position. Without understanding that the money for the program is a grant, only requiring paperwork and time on the part of someone, there is a real inclination to be suspicious.

Matrix # 9—Educating your publics concerning financial matters is a constant and on-going process.

It may be that the principal will have to demonstrate by displaying the paperwork and forms that the program is really totally funded by a grant. Whatever it takes, be prepared to justify your position. Hopefully, the credibility of the administrator is such that the publics do not question the information when presented with documentation.

Hard financial times in a school district will create a frenzy of a free-for-all that turns friend against friend, not unlike a civil war. When budget cuts are contemplated or mandated in the building the principal will need to tread very carefully. With site-based management being what it is, the principal will lead his site-based team in discussions about how dollars can be sliced from the budget. There are all sorts of ways to save money in a building, but the only significant ways to make a real financial impact on the budget is to cutback on, or eliminate staff. This is not what your staff will want to hear, much less discuss in any meaningful way, because they will be talking about people that they see every day. Very few of your teachers will stand up and say "This is a budget crisis and you should eliminate my program and consequently, me."

The principal with guidance from the superintendent will have a target dollar amount in mind that needs to be sliced from the budget. All expenditures should be on the table and open for discussion. Meeting after meeting later, the site-based team will have come up with some ways that the building can save money. These ideas will be put in the form of a recommendation to the superintendent and school board. Try not to let your feelings be hurt, Ms. Principal, but near the top of all the ideas generated to save money will be the suggestion to cut back on or eliminate some administrators.

To prove my point, the following quotes are from each of the school board candidates in Peoria, Illinois, as quoted in the *Peoria Journal Star* prior to the 2005 school board election. There were thirteen candidates and there are thirteen positions taken about the cost of administrators in difficult financial times, which the Peoria School District was experiencing.

"I think we need to look at the rate of pay that the administrators are currently receiving. I do know that administrative salaries are on average higher for this district than in like districts in Illinois."

"There are a few areas that seem duplicated at the administrative level. I would, as a board member, take a close look at this. We also are heavy on the administrative level in comparison to other districts."

"This district has about 20 percent more administrators per student than other districts, 5.3 administrators per 1000 students, and districts of a similar type have 4.3."

"Based on the number of administrators and the number of dollars per student, there should be some room for cuts."

"Everything I've read indicates that, per student, our ratio of administrators to students is more disgraceful than a lot of districts."

"I'd sure like to freeze the top administrative salaries."

"Probably some administrative-types and duties can be cut."

"I would eliminate administrative positions and if feasible ask for a wage freeze."

"You have to make more cuts, but I would look at administrative costs."

"I have some questions in relation to some of the administrative salaries."

"If additional cuts become necessary, I'd like to see a freeze on all administrative salaries, and when administrative positions open, then not filling them at least for one year."

"If cuts must be made, I think we really need to examine the administration."

"I'd cut administrative costs first. Salaries are too high from what I hear from people I talked to when I was getting names (for my petition)."

I have no idea who won the seats on the Peoria board, but the pre-election rhetoric was unanimous, "financially whack the administration."

Your salary as principal is going to be fodder for cost analysis. When this happens to you try not to become emotional and take it personally. Once you cross over into the administrative arena you are no longer one of the teachers, or even an educator in the eyes of some, but the enemy that sucks up too many dollars. As the principal you will be viewed kaleidoscopically, with the teachers endlessly rearranging your shards. As principal expect to have your administrative decisions, salary, and your idiosyncratic ways scrutinized. Keep your persona on the high road and go about your task of taking care of the kids.

Remember if you will, all of those times when you were "just a teacher" and you sat around in the lounge and complained with your cronies about your principal and other administrators, and the fact they were paid so much more than you, for what appeared to you at the time to be a less strenuous and important job than yours. Or, you complained about the endless staff meetings that could have been better handled by a memo; or the fact that your principal was not visible enough, or too visible; or the way your principal played favorites; or the way your principal was constantly changing her mind.

Most of us when we were teachers have at some point vocalized some of these feelings. Maybe it is part of the graveyard humor so necessary to withstand the pressures of the classroom, or possibly your principal really was ineffective in some way.

But just remember, Ms. Principal, that now that you hold the position, you are going to be scrutinized in the same manner in which you have likely scrutinized your former principal. It may not be a pleasant experience, but you must endure it by communicating confidence and being able to take the punches that are thrown at you. Remember this, all principals have at one time been teachers, but very few teachers have ever had the responsibility of being the principal. Just like you once were, they are ignorant of the commitment that it takes to be the leader.

Good communication has been described as "telling people what they want to hear." Teachers and boards of education do not want to hear that there is no money available for such-and-such project or program. A good principal will avoid running out of money in his building at almost any cost.

That sounds so Yoda-ish let's make it a matrix.

Matrix # 10—A good principal will avoid running out of money in his building at almost any cost.

6

Let's Have Funds, Funds, Funds

Now that we have some understanding of how local tax dollars are generated and how states attempt to arrive at an "adequate funding level" through state aid, let's take a look at school accounting systems. The reason that the principal needs to have some familiarity with this is because you will need to make sense of the various reports that are distributed to the administration and the school board. With this knowledge, you as principal, will be able to know exactly how much money your building spent on toilet paper in any given fiscal year.

It would behoove you to take a look at a website prepared by the National Center for Educational Statistics, http://nces.ed.gov. This site will provide you with accounting information for local and state school systems. You will find an extraordinary (at this point overwhelming) amount of data concerning fund numbers; revenue numbers; revenue sources; program expenditure numbers; function numbers for expenditures; object numbers for expenditures; and all sorts of revenue numbers for various revenue funds.

The Government Accounting Standards Board (GASB) has set national accounting principles for state and local governmental bodies. Remember that school districts are governmental bodies. States and school districts have adopted these general revenue and expenditure accounting procedures, known as the Generally Accepted Accounting Procedures (GAAP). There will be a uniform set of budget numbers used in whatever school district you find yourself and the budgeting system is consistent statewide.

School district budgeting really involves two sets of budget numbers within each fund. A fund is simply a set of revenue and expenditures falling into some particular consistent category of related matter.

The GASB suggests the following fund numbers and fund names, as set forth by The National Center for Educational Statistics (NCES):

Fund number	Fund name
10	General Fund
20	Special Revenue Fund
30	Capital Projects Fund
40	Debt Service Fund
45	Permanent Fund
50	Enterprise Fund
55	Internal Revenue Fund
60	Pension Fund
65	Investment Trust Fund
70	Private Purpose Trust Fund
80	Agency Fund
90	Student Activity Fund

It would be helpful if besides just a name for the various funds, we took at look at a more detailed descriptor.

The General Fund accounts primarily for receipts from tax revenue and tuition and the expenditures are for the regular instructional programs and many related activities.

In Texas this describes Fund 199. In New Mexico it is Fund 11000. In Illinois it is known as Fund 10, just as the GAAP recommends. No matter what the number of the fund is in a particular state, the number will be used consistently by each district throughout the state. This same state-by-state difference in numbering can be noted for each of the funds that the states utilize.

The Special Revenue Fund is for legally restricted dollars for a specific purpose such as state and/or federal grants for special education, vocational education, etc.

Capital Projects Fund accounts for revenue for the acquisition or construction of major capital projects.

Debt Service Fund is for the accumulation of receipts for the payment of general long-term debt. Debt service references tax money collected for the payments of bonds or other loans.

Permanent Fund is a new fund for resources given to the district that will benefit it in some way. A donation is the best example.

The <u>Enterprise Fund</u> is the cost of goods and services to provide some service to the public which the public pays for through user charges. The sale of food in the cafeteria is an example.

The <u>Internal Service Fund</u> accounts for operations through which goods or services are sold by the school district to a site-based local unit in the school district or to a local, county, state, or federal government. The charges are on a cost reimbursement basis and not for profit. Examples would be a central supply store or money received from another governmental body, such as money received for a gym or room rental by some group.

<u>Pension Fund</u> is money held in trust for pensions and other employee benefits.

The <u>Investment Trust Fund</u> is for investment pools that the district may be associated with.

<u>Private Purpose Trust Fund</u> is for money that the district receives where the donor specifies that the principal and/or interest is to be used for some specific purpose.

<u>Agency Fund</u> is used by the district for custodial purposes (not janitorial purposes) and involves the receipt of money, temporary investment of money, and payment of said money. Examples are payroll funds, which hold cash; the unemployment trust fund which holds money in reserve for unemployment compensation claims; and student activity funds. The student activity funds are used for money owned and managed by the student body (organizations) under the supervision of a sponsor.

The NCES budget numbering system consists of one set of names and numbers for revenues and one set of names and numbers for expenditures. In the NCES system of accounting the fund numbers are consistent through both revenue and expenditures.

On the revenue side (NCES) there are three sets of numbers. The first two numbers represent the fund into which the revenue is placed. The middle four numbers represent the source of the money for that particular fund, and the last four numbers represent the object for a particular fund.

A typical revenue fund would look like:

<u>Fund</u>	<u>Revenue Sources (or Functions)</u>	<u>Revenue Numbers Objects</u>
XX	XXXX	XXXX

(I am also calling sources, functions, because some states do. Remember this is only the NCES model.) before the proper numbers are placed in. We already have seen what the fund numbers are and the fund names. One of the most used revenue funds will be '10,' the general fund. This is where (typically) all tax revenue and state aid is placed.

The NCES system uses revenue source numbers 1100 through 5700.

Revenue Numbers (Functions)

1000 series (1100–1990) is revenue from various local sources

2000 series is revenues from intermediate sources

3000 series is revenues from state sources

4000 series is revenues from federal sources

5000 series is revenues from other financing sources

For example, the local tax levy revenues are source or function number 1110. How do we know this? It is on the chart of the NCES.

Revenue accounting also will have a third set of four numbers referencing what is generally called the 'object.' Object numbers look like function or source numbers but they fix into different funds based on the descriptor of what the object is.

In our example of local tax revenue, which goes into fund number 10 (the general fund) and under function or source number 1110, it has an object code in the general fund of 1110 (also). So the revenue accounting code for our local property tax collection going into the general fund would be:

10-1110-1110. Simply put, under the NCES model, this is local tax money placed into the general education fund. Typically the NCES model does not use object numbers for revenue accounts, only for the expenditure accounts. Several states have a similar format.

My assumption is that all of the fifty states have a similar financial coding structure based on the NCES model. This is only an assumption because only someone with too much time on his hands would bother to look up the exact coding system in a state that did not matter to him. Of the states that I am familiar with all have a NCES model, but there may be more or fewer numbers in the fund-function-object columns and the descriptors can be different.

Following is the New Mexico list of revenue funds and a descriptor of the fund.

Fund Number	Descriptor
11000 Operational Fund	Money to educate students Pk-12
13000 Transportation	Transportation of students
14000 State Textbooks	State provided dollars for textbooks
21000 Student Nutrition	Federal dollars for lunch/breakfast
22000 Athletics	Cost of running the athletic programs
23000 Activity	Funds generated by students for students
24000 Federal Grants	Categorical federal grants
25000 Local/State Grants	Categorical local and state grants
31100 Bond Building	Sale of bonds for building/remodeling
31700 Capital Improvements	Building/remodeling supported by local levy
41000 Debt Service	Repayment of bonds

You can compare New Mexico's funds with the NCES model and descriptors and obviously see many similarities, but also some differences. Rest assured that every type of school district revenue will be properly coded somewhere.

Let's see if we can muddy the waters with one more set of revenue fund accounts, this time from Illinois.

Fund number	Descriptor
10 Education Fund	Salaries/supplies for professional staff
20 Operations/Maintenance	Cost of building operations
30 Bond and Interest Fund	Revenue of bonds
40 Transportation Fund	Cost of buses, drivers, repairs, etc.
50 Municipal Retirement Fund	Money collected for teacher retirement
60 Site and Construction	Cost of renovation and building
70 Working Cash Fund	A specific tax levy Illinois
80 Rent Fund	Money collected for renting facilities
90 Fire Prevention and Safety	A special levy for safety improvements

Compare Illinois to New Mexico and the NCES model. All have something called "funds" and each of the funds is assigned a number and a descriptor. Although there are differences there are similarities. Texas has well over 250 different funds in which revenue can be placed and from which expenditures will be taken. It is not as cumbersome as it first may appear, but needless to say, it takes a larger 'Financial Coding Manual' and some getting used to by the folk that have to deal with it. We have defined "fund" before but let's do it again in a different way.

A fund is an independent accounting entity with its own assets, liabilities, and fund balances. Funds are established to account for the financing of specific activities of the district's operations. Revenue accounts will have corresponding numbers for the expenditure accounts. Remember that this is double-entry bookkeeping. Think of the funds, if you will, as many check books.

There will be a revenue account, let's say, 10-1100-001, which is for local property tax collection. '10' we have found is typically the number assigned to the general education fund, of which salaries are a major component (even Texas begins this much utilized fund with the number '1,' as the main fund number in Texas is 199). When salaries are paid for the teachers in September, there will be a withdrawal from the revenue account (10-1100-001). Because we are paying salaries, we have an expenditure account that corresponds to the revenue account number, only found in the expenditure section of the budget. Trust me on this; the expenditure numbers (fund-function-object) are legion compared to the number of revenue account numbers.

Why? Think of the following example using the Illinois Fund 10. Supplies for teachers come from this revenue account. When we expend the money for supplies we don't just mix elementary, middle school, high school, vocational, physical education, business, etc. all into one pot. Oh no. Each department in each school or each area in each school has their supply budget. Why do we do this? The district must account for where the dollars are spent. We are not spending "our" money. It is taxpayer money of some form or another.

So then, if we use the Illinois revenue account number of 10-1100-001, some typical expenditure account objects would be:

Expenditure Account	Descriptor
401	Elementary music
402	Elementary physical education
403	Elementary guidance supplies
404	Office supplies—elementary

When a school board member, administrator, teacher, or a member of the public looks at a listing of the bills paid for a particular month they will see an account number for each of the expenditures.

The expenditure number will link back to a revenue account from which the expenditure will be paid. In Texas the expense line for supplies for a school district's dyslexia services would be 199-11-6399. This lets the reader know that the money is coming from Fund 199—The General Fund; Function 11—The Instruction Function; and Object 6399.

The first two digits of the object number tells the enlightened viewer that any number in the 6300 series will be dealing with supplies and materials, therefore, 6399 will be concerned with supplies or materials of some nature.

Texas breaks this dyslexia expense further down with a fourth set of numbers which tell us the sub-object. This sub-object is an optional management tool that is not reported to the state capitol in Austin. A fifth set of numbers gives the organizational code, which is used when a cost is clearly attributable to a specific organization. A sixth number tells which fiscal year this budget is reporting on and is mandatory in Texas. The seventh set of numbers in Texas is the Program Intent and describes what it is, numbers that identify a specific program to which the money is targeted.

Supplies for dyslexia services in this particular school in Texas would be coded as expense item 199-11-6399-34-001-4-9900.

From what revenue account will the dyslexia supplies be taken? This is much simpler than figuring out the expenditure code. The answer in Texas is 199-11, the general fund and the function of instruction.

Most of you won't give much of a rip about this if you are reading it outside of the state of Texas. That's okay because the same basic principles are going to be present in your state. Get your hands on the state's 'Financial Coding Manual.' The bookkeeper is certain to have one.

Expenditure account numbers and examples could go on for many pages. There is no need to bore you further. Enough to say, if there is $500,000 budgeted district wide for supplies, that money may be distributed in countless ways throughout the school system.

Each and every way that it is distributed will have a specific expenditure account number all of its very own. The middle school principal will be able to tell on January 15, as an example, out of the $500 budgeted for toilet paper for her school, that $721 has already been spent. Oh no! Crisis time. Call the superintendent; take the issue to the school board. What do we do after our supply of toilet paper on hand is exhausted? (Exhausted sounds like the right word.)

Let's save the answer to this very real and distressing question for Chapter 7.

It is vital for the principal at some point in the first few weeks of a new job, to find whatever they call the 'Chart of Accounts,' the 'Account Structure,' the 'Code of Accounts Handbook,' the 'Programming Accounting Manual,' or whatever the heck it is called in the state in which you find yourself. This manual, no matter what name it goes under, will provide you with the fund-function-object structure and give you the definitions of all the terms. We come to another *Matrix*, which is a variation of *Matrix # 2—If you don't know the answer—find someone who does.*

MATRIX # 11—If you can not find what you are looking for in your office, just figure that your disgruntled predecessor trashed it or stole it, and go ask for a new one.

How important is it really for the principal to have this manual? Remember that I have calculated that the principal will work on the budget approximately 3% of his school-year time in a ridiculously assumed eight-hour day. The accounting manual of which I speak, and you seek, will come in handy only on the occasion where you may need to specify a specific expenditure number to the bookkeeper. This does happen. Find the shelf space for it.

A working knowledge of revenue and expenditure accounts also helps when you are looking at the district budget and monthly financial reports for the district and your particular building. With time and practice you will become familiar with it, just about the time you change jobs and find yourself in a new state with a different configuration. But take heart, once you can determine what an Angus cow looks like you can look at a Texas Longhorn and although recognizing the differences, you will find many similarities and still be able to tell it is a cow (of sorts).

I had to become tangentially familiar with the Texas Financial Accountability System due to the fact that I get students from Texas in my finance class at Eastern New Mexico University. Texas has over 250 different categories of funds.

In Texas there is a mandatory 3 digit code for the fund (pick one of the 257), followed by a function code, an object code and then several optional codes that districts in Texas have available for use.

Following the object code there is the availability for an organizational code, which identifies the unit of organization, such as high school, middle school, elementary school, principal's office at the elementary school, etc. The object code is followed by the fiscal year code and we know what that means. Fiscal year 06 is here as this book is published in July 2005 so current revenue accounts will have 06 in this slot. And if we do not have enough numbers yet in our Texas system, the schools can add a 'program intent code', which are used to pinpoint the cost of instruction for a program directed toward a particular need of a specific set of students. Basic physics might be classified 11, for example.

This is what a Texas account code would look like:

Fund	Function	Object	Organization	FY	Program
xxx	xx	xxxx	xxx	6	xx

Perhaps when people from Texas say that everything is bigger in Texas they are more correct than they know. I do believe, however, that we can still recognize this revenue system as a 'cow.'

Keep in mind that revenue is deposited in the 'revenue accounts.' Revenues have very specific accounts into which they are placed based on the criteria of the state department of education of the fifty states. Expenditures are paid out of expenditure accounts that once again have very specific accounting codes found in the individual state's school fiscal accounting manuals.

If your district bookkeeper has been looking after the day-to-day fiscal matters of the school for any length of time, he is likely to have memorized many of the coding accounts. Also, computer generated bookkeeping packages have not made the task of maintaining fiscal order any simpler, but they have certainly made it quicker. It is possible through computer financial packages to have access to practically any and all school district financial information.

Do you want to know how much your cafeteria spent for plastic plates last year? We can find that out. Would you like to know the escalating price of the cost to provide gasoline for all district athletic events over the past five years? We can find that out.

Thirty-one years ago in 1974 when I began my school administrative run, it was the dark age of information. The computer has not always been around. All the financial data was kept in written ledger form, which made it very cumbersome and time consuming to ferret out. Frankly, I do not remember how revenue and expenditures were even coded back then. The National Center for Educational Statistics and the Government Accounting Standards Board set of accounting funds, with all the deviations of the same found in the fifty states, did not exist.

7

Toilet Paper Crisis

You are out of toilet paper at the middle school and your toilet paper budget is gone. What has likely happened is that your disgruntled predecessor took all of the excess rolls from the last fiscal year to his new job? Probably not. In actuality, your toilet paper supply budget was likely not established at a high enough figure to cover the needs of the building.

How is a new principal to know how much toilet paper to order and budget for? You won't, but your head custodian or whoever orders your building supplies should know the inventory left over in May and how much was ordered the past summer. If fifty gross were ordered last summer and there are six rolls of paper left, then he knows (or you know) that 7,194 rolls of toilet paper were used in the middle school. Six rolls remaining is cutting it pretty close to the limit. Probably too close, because there may be summer school and events where people are using the bathroom.

Perhaps you should order fifty-one gross this summer. What you should not do, in a brilliant cost-cutting measure designed to impress your superintendent, is order thirty gross and hope for the best. This will cause you to run out, perhaps as early as January 15.

Do not call the superintendent and tell him that you are out of toilet paper. This will be something of a concern to the superintendent, only when he gets calls from very disgruntled teachers and parents. Your job as principal is to solve the problem before the superintendent gets calls.

Do not address the school board with this concern, unless you are a comedian. If you feel the need to be comedic with the board be sure and wear a red rubber nose in the process. This will solidify their opinion of you.

Also, I do not advocate sending a letter home to the parents asking that toilet paper be sent to school with their children. This was the major topic of discussion at the local coffee watering holes (and ultimately at the school board meeting) when a principal actually did this.

What you will do is find the necessary resources to buy more toilet paper; either through the transfer of money from one of your accounts to another, or take the plunge and order more toilet paper and go over budget in that expense account. Going over budget is known as "going in the red."

Going into the red is not good business for a building or school district. Your superintendent will spend great quantities of his time worrying about financial matters. You as a first-year principal won't. As a principal there are just certain things that have to be taken care of whether or not you have the money readily available in a particular account. Toilet paper is one of those things.

I once had a group of teachers' approach me concerning the toilet paper being too rough. They were displeased that I, or someone, had found it necessary to purchase such cheap toilet paper. It seems, and I took their word for this, that it was causing a skin irritation. My solution out of a whole array of possibilities, some of which were not appropriate to express, was for them to bring their own stockpile from home.

Here is another example of an item that you must find the money for. You began the fiscal year with a textbook budget (to be used for new and refurbishing books) of $25,000. However, now it is March and three new students have moved into the building, all enrolling in advanced calculus. There is no more money in the textbook budget and there are no extra calculus books in the district. What does a prudent principal do?

Do you inform the family and the students that advanced calculus is closed to them? Do you allow the students to enter the class, but they must share a book with an existing student of the class? Do you ask the teacher to make copies of the book on the duplicating machine for the three new students? Do you order your secretary to make the copies, or do you make them yourself? Do you call around to another school district and see if any of these books are available?

You might do the latter, but you will find the three calculus textbooks some way or the money to purchase them. Why? Think it over. This is what we are all about, providing an education to the students. Just be thankful that the students enrolling into your building are advanced calculus students. They could be a different type of student entirely.

New students needing textbooks that are not available with any money to procure them calls for what I refer to as a 'contingency of the unexpected.' The unexpected will happen to you as principal regularly, and often the unexpected will be of a financial nature.

MATRIX # 12—Have a contingency plan always and in financial matters have a 'contingency account fund.'

Some schools will actually have an account called 'contingency' and it can be used for items such as toilet paper and calculus books. An account of this type would be helpful for the principal, but you will need permission from the superintendent and then form a special accounting number with the bookkeeper. (This is likely too ambitious for your first year.)

Once again, to get the necessary textbooks you will either go over your allotted textbook budget or transfer money from some other account that is not utilizing all of the allocated dollars.

This is tricky. As a new principal you do not ask the basketball coach of thirty-years if he would be willing to do with five less of the dozen new basketballs that he has budgeted for, because you need the money for calculus textbooks.

It is never wise to take someone else's money for your own purposes. Although all the district money flows from "one big sucking straw" (see Chapter 4), teachers obtain (in their minds at least) ownership of what they perceive to be their budgeted money. A fifth-grade teacher would rather spend his allocated supply dollars on a world globe that glows in the dark, spins by remote control, and hums "it's a small world after all" rather than "let the allocated supply budget go unspent."

As principal you will have to determine if such a globe is necessary and not authorize it just because the money has been allocated. Or better yet, what about letting a teacher buy a mini-refrigerator for his classroom to keep his soda cold? When you question the purchase order for this mini-fridge, as you should, the rationale will not be that this is for his soda. Teachers are much too clever. He will tell you it is to keep the kids' milk cool, or to store popsicles for special treats, or keep Billy's medicine cool. You will need to be on your toes and make some decisions as to what is "best for kids." It may be trite, but all budget allocations need to keep the kids foremost in mind.

Let's revisit our teacher that wants cold soda and yogurt at his beck and call and is too lazy to walk to the teachers' workroom for it (editorial comment). Do we okay the purchase order because the mini-refrigerator costs $109 and he has $500 in his supply account? I don't know what you will do, but I know for sure that Billy's medicine should be housed in the office or with the nurse, not in a classroom refrigerator.

As principal you can do as you wish, but I will guarantee you three things. First of all, if one teacher gets a refrigerator for his classroom there will be several more requests for mini-fridges for other classrooms. Secondly, if you sign and pass this purchase order on to the superintendent (particularly in smaller districts the superintendent signs off on all purchase orders) you get to put her on the spot. As a new principal do not put your superintendent on the spot. Thirdly, do you really want to explain to the superintendent and school board why you purchased twenty mini-refrigerators? I didn't think so.

MATRIX # 13 (if you believe in unlucky numbers this is a really momentous matrix)—Do not knowingly place your superintendent on a financial hot spot.

As a beginning principal, what sort of financial responsibilities might be expected in the first two weeks on the job? In Chapter 8, I am going to discuss budget building in some detail, but truthfully, by the time you come on board as the first-year principal on July 1, or more typically August 1, your budget should be fundamentally settled. The key word here is "should." The superintendent or business manager has been "on top of" the fiscal year budget ending on June 30 for months and will have a thorough direction for what is anticipated to happen in the coming fiscal year.

If staff had to be eliminated in your building that will have taken place prior to your arrival. Next spring, however, you as principal will be expected to have input into personnel decisions for the following fiscal year, whether staff will be eliminated, increased, or transferred. As a seasoned principal (after one month on the job) you should always to be thinking about the financial future of your building and consequently the district finances.

Money or the lack of money primarily, impacts your building in ways that from being a former teacher you can understand, but being the principal in charge of the building compounds the issue of diminishing funds. Think of morale issues when the district has financial needs. Rotten morale affects the quality of instruction and makes a formerly happy place to work a den of gripe. It is a platitude that "teachers are in the business for the love of the kids (a missionary mentality)," but don't bet on this particularly when strong teacher unions are involved in financial contract disputes.

In the first two weeks on the job, you might expect to find left over purchase orders for your consideration. This is a dirty trick perpetrated on you by the former principal of the building, but it is likely to happen. Some of the POs can wait until you gather the information that is necessary to make your decision. Some POs you cannot dally around with. If the deadline to get your math books sent in to be rebound and back in time for the beginning of school in the fall is July 5, then you had better take action.

But how will the principal know what the deadline is for the rebinding company? Do you have any idea? Common sense should indicate that this purchase order has some time sensitivity to it. Perhaps you will have an experienced secretary who will leave you a memo with the purchase order. Perhaps you will get a visit or phone call from the math teacher, because this will be of particular concern to him or her. Just hope you find out these crucial things someway somehow, because as Betty Davis said in *All About Eve,* I paraphrase with liberties, *"Hang on, it is going to be a bumpy ride, now that you are principal."*

Do not be surprised if you have a plethora of callers during your first few days on the job. Many of these callers will be from your staff seeking information from you and wanting their particular financial issues addressed.

My first week on the job as a beginning principal the entire special education staff of my building (all two of them) came calling demanding aides for their classrooms. How in the world would they expect me to know? But they did. I didn't. I didn't specifically know the special education situation that they found themselves in, in terms of the number of students that they were responsible for.

I do not think that they really expected me to authorize the hiring of an aide on the spot. They did expect me to listen to them, which I did. I listened to them until they were ready to stop. I gave them my time and took the request under advisement.

MATRIX # 14—As with most considerations, give those with issues that impact finance your undivided attention; promise to consider the issue; consider the issue in the manner it deserves; and get back as soon as possible with your response.

8

Building Your School Budget

Every school finance book that I have ever seen will tell you that a district budget must have a philosophical base and the dollars available should be spent around the philosophies. This is probably good advice for any individual or organization. We all need to have some supporting rationale or plan about how we will toss our money around.

Philosophically the individual might premise his budget with statements such as, "I am not going to go into debt." "I will pay my credit cards off monthly." "I will save 5% of every paycheck." Whatever.

Following are some commonly shared philosophical beliefs that I have used to preface my school and district budgets:

1. All children can and will learn.

2. Learning takes place when children are <u>active</u> participants rather than passive observers.

3. Successful teachers and administrators must be models, coaches, facilitators, team players, observers, learners, and risk takers.

4. Learners are problem solvers, strategists, and risk takers.

5. Children must be encouraged to constantly seek excellence and teachers must do everything possible to make that happen.

6. Active student learning is enhanced through cooperative learning.

7. Parents must be encouraged to play an active role in every classroom.

What sources I plagiarized those principles from, I have no idea, but they seem rather universal and make sense, to me at least. But just how do our "beliefs" translate into the budget? In any number of ways.

Take "all children can and will learn" for example. If you believe that elementary children learn best in a classroom environment with a ratio of no more than fifteen students to one teacher, and this is your priority, then it will cost you more money to implement this philosophy rather than one that says, "a good first grade teacher can educate thirty students in a classroom just fine."

If the district's philosophy states that children should be active participants then the budget should include "hands-on" types of supplies rather than more passive items such as workbooks.

If you wish to encourage parents to be active in the education of their children, then dollars will be allocated to inspire that association. The actual budget reflects in dollars and cents the philosophy and policies of the district, reflecting the efforts of the school board to provide for a good educational program.

School boards exist to provide a good, sound educational program consistent with the district's financial ability. Adequate salary schedules have to be maintained in order to keep and employ good teachers and other staff members. At the very least, the district has to be competitive with surrounding districts. The school board also has to maintain and improve the physical facilities to enhance the function of instruction. I have seen buckets lining hallways and classrooms to catch the water from leaks in the roof. This is not conducive to instruction.

The school board also must plan and implement a program to ensure that the pupil population has what they need to learn, yet at the same time keep in mind that there will be future school budgets. What I mean by this is that the future must be considered when spending resources. It might be nice to drive a Cadillac, but you will also need to consider future gas purchases.

Silly me. As superintendent I made a horrible mistake once (actually I made this mistake several times and it bit me once) of employing an English teacher with twenty-seven years of experience and a master's degree. She was a fantastic teacher. All agreed that she was fantastic, children, parents, other teachers, community members, the principal, and board members. It could not have been more unanimous that she was magnificent. I hired her for $48,000 a year during flush times. What I should have done was hire a $19,000 beginning teacher. Look at all the money that I could have saved the district over three years. I was, however, committed to employing the best teachers that we could find. As I say, silly me. I had an inappropriate philosophy. I should have opted to employ the best least expensive teacher possible.

One reviewer of this book thought that the above paragraph illustrating my financial misjudgment had a tinge of bitterness. Upon reflection the reviewer is correct, although I prefer the word 'resentful.' Not having the financial resources to do what is best for the students can have a tendency to disappoint me and other worthwhile administrators.

It just seems so simple to say that before you spend money you should have some idea of how you want to spend it. This, of course, is true, but the reality is that there are certain costs that will be common to all schools. When you think about schools you think about teachers. You have to budget for teachers. It is estimated that the budget is anywhere from 75% to 85% tied up in the salaries and benefits of the teachers. This fact would not seem to leave you with much philosophical financial wiggle room. And it doesn't.

For example, it might be pedagogically wonderful to place in the budget dollars so that every child in the district or building could receive a laptop computer to utilize during the school day and take home at night. Many schools may aspire to this goal; few will have the money to actually implement it. It was always my dream to implement a foreign language program in the early elementary grades as research tells us that this is the best time to introduce students to another language. Alas, in the districts that I was employed in we had to cut a foreign language in the high school we were so poor. There was never any consideration of foreign language instruction in the lower elementary grades.

So philosophy and reality do collide sometimes, but then again we all are under the mandate that "no child will be left behind." Is it any wonder that one of the major complaints about this legislation is that there is not enough money to support it?

Complaining is not going to get us anywhere, so let's continue with our budget building.

Many textbooks will tell you that one way to build a budget is to base your budget on previous budgets. This is certainly one way to begin and will give you a good base as to where to start. For example, if from the financial report, you see that $10,000 was budgeted for copy paper for your middle school last year and as of June 30 (the end of the past fiscal year) there was $1,800 left in that particular line item then you will know that there should be some unused inventory somewhere in your building or district.

So how much money should I budget for copy paper this year? Factor in your philosophies and realities. Did you add a first-grade teacher to decrease pupil-teacher ratios? Did you eliminate two teachers because of declining enrollment or financial problems? Is your philosophy going to be that teachers are restricted in the amount of copies that they may make and you intend to reduce usage of the copy machine because we all know that there is much more of a cost to making copies that just the paper costs? What is the cost of copy paper going to be this year? Will I be able to get more for fewer dollars, or is it going to cost me more to get the same amount of paper?

These are examples of considerations to acknowledge when thinking about something as simple as how much money should I budget for copy paper. Just comparing budgets of previous years is an unsatisfactory procedure when used as the only factor in evaluating the needs of your building.

Having been critical of "only" looking at the previous year's budget does not mean that you should not utilize it. You need a copy of your building's previous budget. Utilizing the previous fiscal budget leads to the 'line-item budget;' this is referred to as an object-of-expenditure budget. Line-item budgeting is in fact what budgets look like. Let's look at this abbreviated example for a middle school of what a line-item budget would look like (minus the fund-function-object coding) as of July 1 for the past FY.

Budget category	Budgeted Current Year	Remaining	Proposed Budget
Salaries/Teachers	$471,225	$2,987	
Salaries/Office	$124,000	$871	
Supplies/Art	$1,000	($1,541)	
Postage/Office	$5,500	$180	

What can we extrapolate from the above four examples? The first two examples of salaries are typically very predictable because you know by August 1 who your staff will be and what their salaries will be. You also know that all of this money is going to be provided to you by the central office. There is always the unforeseeability of late resignations, transfers, or positions not filled, but typically you can come very close. There shouldn't be too many surprises in the course of a school year. Just be sure you factor in any salary increases for the coming year and longetivity steps if they exist in your building.

When you see parentheses around a dollar amount it is commonly understood that the item has gone over budget. This is the case with our example of art supplies, which went $541 over budget. There may be numerous explanations from which to choose for why this happened, and as principal you may have to select one, but what should you do about next year's budget? This is going to depend on the reason for the over budget. Were additional art classes added? Did the kiln quit working in the middle of the year and a new one had to be purchased? Did vandals break into the art room and destroy the paints? Who knows what happened, but an item going over budget is going to be viewed as a lack of foresight on the part of the budget builder. And because of the rush to site-based budgets, that ultimate building budget builder is going to be the principal.

MATRIX # 15—No matter how powerfully you contemplate the budget, there is still a lot of guesswork involved in the final product.

That matrix is not there to make you feel better. It is there because it is the truth. Things happen during the year over which you have no control, such as our toilet paper crisis. Your obligation is to do the best you can and take every factor into consideration. A superintendent and school board can ask nothing more of a neophyte principal. And when you really consider it, you are not really a novice at all. Certainly you have worked with classroom budgets. Perhaps you are an ex-coach and had to deal with your athletic budget. All of that experience will put you in good stead. (In addition you have taken a class on finance and you are reading this book.)

What I always did as a principal was display my budget using the financial coding system and a line item with an explanation that would satisfy those that knew nothing about the budget. What follows is an example from my building expenditure budget in Illinois, using the Illinois accounting structure (which is for illustrative purposes only) and the explanations that I gave.

Account Number	Amount	Explanation
16.10.1130.2150	$45,125	District's share of early retirement incentive
16.10.1400.5041	$25,000	Vocational equipment repair and new table saw
16.40.1110.4200	$43,200	new fourth grade mathematics textbooks
16.10.1900.0000	$10,000	to augment the Truancy Grant
16.10.1432.2213	$845	Weekly Readers—grade 3

The account number won't mean anything to the school board, or most anyone else, but the amount and explanation should be clear so that anyone can understand where your money is budgeted.

Without the explanation handy in <u>your</u> budget can you imagine someone asking you "out of the blue" why you over spent on line item '16.10.1432.2213' by $8.53? Trust me once again; I have had officious school board members want to know why some line item was over budget by an amount that miniscule. The number means nothing, but the explanation tells you everything. Your bookkeeper can always tell you exactly what '16.10.1432.2213' is and means, but why bother him every time. Know your own building's financial business. Have a copy of the Financial Accounting Manual in your office for handy reference and readily refer to it when necessary.

Even better, be proactive and give your superintendent, staff, school board, and anyone else who wants one a copy of your building budget with explanations. They may still ask you why you went over $8.53 for 3rd grade Weekly Readers, but they will know at least it was for Weekly Readers, and because it was Weekly Readers that may stop the question before it is asked.

A few paragraphs ago I mentioned 'site-based budgeting.' Site-based budgeting (SBB) is a management theory that deserves some additional explanation as a concept, although SBB is really what we have been discussing.

SBB is the notion that a district budget is comprised of many different parts and should be developed at the building level with the involvement of the people that are most impacted by the budget. This is obviously a decentralized system which provides a way of allocating revenue for instructional supplies, materials, equipment, textbooks, library books, etc., to each of the specific buildings in the district. SBB necessitates that the building principal along with her staff match the available dollar resources with the needs of students in that building.

In large school districts with multiple elementary schools or middle schools, you can easily see the advantage of SBB. Brimley and Garfield list what they see as five benefits of site-based management:

1. Enables site participants to exert substantial influence on school policy decisions.

2. Enhances employee morale and motivation.

3. Strengthens the quality of schoolwide planning processes.

4. Fosters the development of characteristics associated with effective schools.

5. Improves the academic achievement of students.[8]

PPB dovetails very nicely with PPBS. Abbreviations can be so much fun to use, but consider *Matrix # 3* again. Be sure that you thoroughly explain your terms, as not everyone will understand them, particularly the acronyms. In fact, why do you use acronyms at all? Oh sure, some such as F.B.I. have become entrenched into common understanding wherever you go and may save some breath of the speaker, but less unacquainted concepts such as PPBS should be discussed using the full name of 'Planning, Programming, Budgeting System' (PPBS).

The 'Planning, Programming, Budgeting System' is a budgeting program of objectives, a plan, and a schedule of periodic reviews listed by budget categories. Line item budgets are developed by site-based teams to achieve the objectives and plans of the PPBS.

Just think of the good feeling you are going to have about yourself as the principal when you finish your budget and are able to monitor it continuously throughout the school year. The reality will always be that you will have only so many discretionary dollars to allocate. Allocate wisely based on what is best for the students of your building.

I employed a principal several years ago who placed $12,000 of his discretionary dollars into an account for 'student attendance incentives.' This particular building, which was a middle school, had an absentee rate of 6%, which his site-based team felt needed to be reduced and was indeed over state average. This was a district of 1,500 students so I as superintendent included myself on the site-based team. In retrospect that was likely too intimidating for some and a mistake. This particular principal gave away bicycles, music disks, t-shirts, free trips, etc. for improved attendance. Great idea and absenteeism was reduced in his building.

Here is the sad part of the story. When the money crunch arrives it will be successful programs like this that are slashed from the budget. It's true that the better your attendance rate the more state aid you will receive; therefore it would seem to be in everyone's best interest to continue with a program of this sort if it can be demonstrated that it is having a positive effect.

In this case the teachers elected to put the money back into the salary pool rather than into attendance incentives for the pupils. Rightly or wrongly, that is site-based management, and PPB systems.

9

Sundry Other Stuff

There are going to be other 'money matter' issues that the beginning principal will need to deal with almost from the very beginning of the school year. I will discuss a few of these concerns.

The first issue that will likely surface, probably even before school actually begins, will involve ticket sales for athletic events. The good news is once again that as a former teacher you are familiar with this and may in fact have been a ticket taker yourself. As a teacher, however, you were likely only responsible for picking up the change box and tickets, making correct change, tearing the tickets in half, and turning over the money and tickets to someone at the end of the event. You did not have to worry about where the change or tickets came from.

As principal, you now have to make sure that there is a change box, or boxes as the case may be. Typically, the district bookkeeper (building secretary, if authorized, or you, the principal, if authorized) will write a check for 'cash' to the admissions account, get the check cashed, and *voila*; there is your change for the big game. The amount of change money you get will depend on the expected patronage at the event. If you don't know what to expect see *MATRIX # 2*.

As the beginning principal you might get lucky and be employed in a district that has an athletic director who organizes all of this activity and will leave you off the hook, but you might not. Often beginning principals find themselves "starting small" in districts and schools without all of the personnel amenities, such as an athletic director.

I have been amazed at how many principals have told me that they do not use tickets for athletic events. How then, can there ever be an accounting of the money? If you know that you begin the evening with $500 in change, and the bank says that $2,135 was deposited, how will you know how many people attended the event? You won't without one-half of the ticket in order to verify the sales. Schools charge more for adults than children. At least two different colored tickets are usually involved. With tickets you can count the number of ticket stubs of both groups. If you deposited $2,135 and you began with $500 in change, then you know that you grossed $1,635 at the event. If you charge $5 per adult and you have 273 red adult ticket stubs then you know that there was $1,365 in adult sales. That leaves $270 in blue ticket stubs, which are the children tickets. If the blue tickets are $2 each, then 135 children entered the gates. There should be 135 blue ticket stubs. Very simple.

Do not expect it to be that simple at a large event. Ticket takers give back the wrong change (not every ticket taker is a mathematics teacher), ticket takers forget in the rush to give out a ticket or tear a ticket. All of these things can happen so that the ticket stubs and gate receipts do not balance.

What does the principal do? If the actual receipts and ticket sales are off slightly, probably nothing, except monitor it. If the two are off substantially there is a problem that needs to be addressed.

If you should walk into a situation where tickets are not used, change the policy. Without tickets there is no defense for the ticket takers, or whoever ultimately ends up depositing the money, if someone should make accusations of mishandling the gate receipts. No defense whatsoever; you simply cannot prove your innocence. Don't place yourself or anyone else in that position. Also, ticket stubs provide proof of paid admission for attendees.

As principal make sure that at least two things occur:

1. Use prenumbered tickets to control admission which will enable someone to reconcile the money with the number of tickets sold.

2. At the end of the event, someone in charge must secure the funds. Best-case scenario is to deposit the money in a night deposit box.

The district should have a policy established determining how much money can be locked in the office at night. No amount of money over $50 should be left in the office over night, but that is a building or district decision.

As principal, make sure that your staff understands that they are not to leave money in their rooms, and I do not mean just over night. Teachers collect all sorts of money at certain times and it needs to be sent immediately to the office. No exception, no excuse will be accepted.

Petty cash funds are typically a topic of concern for beginning principals. Petty cash funds cover unexpected expenditures, and as the name suggests, this is a fund that is established by board policy.

Petty cash is a small amount of money that is available to staff for reimbursement for very inexpensive emergency purchases. The benefit of petty cash as an emergency tool is that the staff member does not go through the purchase order procedure.

For example, it is after school and the director of the play needs an electric extension cord. Typically, he would fill out a PO for $7.50, get all the signatures and then purchase his electric extension cord. This is an unexpected emergency; he needs one now and it is after hours.

The petty cash fund comes in handy because the director can purchase the cord with his own dollars, take the receipt for the electric cord to the office tomorrow and be reimbursed the $7.50. The play director does not have to wait until the school board meets and approves the bills for the reimbursement of the $7.50. At the school board meeting the board will approve the $7.50 that was spent for petty cash.

How much money should be kept in a petty cash fund? I would suggest no more than $50.00.

As a new principal, if your school has an existing petty cash fund, find out the policies and procedures that regulate it.

If your school does not have a petty cash fund you will need to determine first of all if you think you need one, and secondly you will need to obtain permission to begin one. This permission will entail working through the superintendent and the district's financial officer, likely to be the bookkeeper located in the central office.

Here are a couple of other tips about the petty cash fund. The procedures regarding the fund should be placed in the staff handbook and discussed at the opening of school building meeting when the handbook is detailed to the staff. Do this so that everyone knows that you do not go to the petty cash fund to get a small personal check cashed, neither do you 'borrow' from the fund to buy lunch or a soda. Always insist on receipts from any money dispersed from the fund.

The petty cash fund is a convenience to the staff. As the principal, you will determine if you want to continue the fund or implement one.

What happens when there is no money left in the petty cash fund or it is running low? The answer is that it is reauthorized back to the original figure, but because it is strictly an emergency account, I would expect this reauthorization only annually. If the petty cash fund is being depleted you either did not authorize enough to begin with, or your staff lacked the foresight to avoid emergencies.

Do not confuse the petty cash fund with a 'change fund.' A change fund is established as a temporary fund that will have a constant dollar amount in it at all times. It will have a constant dollar amount because it is not used for any reimbursement purposes, as the petty cash fund is, but is used only to make change when someone purchases something like a candy bar, a pencil, an admission ticket, or a raffle ticket that the student council or some other school organization is selling.

If $10.00 is given to the student council sponsor for the purpose of making change for candy sales, the amount of money in the student council change fund is always $10.00.

At the same time the student council is selling candy bars, the After School Bible Club is selling Bibles. The ASBC will also have a change box. (The principal needs to ask herself if the ASBC should be selling Bibles on campus.)

There may be many change funds in operation at any one time, but there is only one petty cash fund and that is controlled in the office by the principal.

You may be asking where the money comes from for these organization change funds. The money comes from the individual organization accounts. If the student council needs money for making change for their candy sales then the sponsor writes a check to 'cash' from that account and once again a mini account has been created. When the sales of candy are finished, the $10.00 is deposited back into the student council account.

These change boxes should not be kept in classrooms at night or after the selling has stopped. Neither should they be kept in a student's locker. Students are typically the ones doing the selling and making the change and the convenient thing to do may be to put the change box in a locker, but this should not ever happen.

As we discussed previously, the change box for athletic events needs to be deposited after the event. $500 in the athletic event change box is quite different than the $10.00 in the student council change box.

Parent organizations and booster clubs often engage in major fund-raising activities. In turn, they will provide much needed materials and equipment that the regular school budget could not otherwise afford.

Parental groups are independent and the funds they are able to raise are private. The principal has no fiscal responsibility. It is possible that because you are the principal that the parental groups will look to you for some financial guidance. The best tip that I can provide is to make sure, to the extent that you can, that the treasurer of the organization is adept enough to do what is expected. As principal, you might think about offering some bookkeeping training to any parental organization that requests it. Generously advertise this 'free' training. This will send a signal that you, the principal have financial matters and good accounting procedures as a top priority in the building. This does not mean that the principal has to provide the actual training. All organizations should be aware that they are subject to an audit.

The principal sets the financial tone for her building from the beginning by communicating high expectations regarding money matters. The teachers' handbook should clearly detail the purchase order process that you expect. I suggest that nothing be ordered without a purchase order signed by the teacher making the request and the principal. There should be no exceptions to this rule. Inform the teachers that if they purchase something without procuring the proper signature and following the proper paper channels, that the item belongs to them and they will be expected to pay for it. The district will not cover the purchase of any item that does not follow procedure.

Once upon a time there was a science teacher that forgot the purchase order process and ordered several lab kits to be used in an archeology unit. When the kits arrived with a bill of $300 and no traceable PO, it was clear enough who had ordered them and that procedures had not been followed.

Does the principal okay the purchase and write a PO after the fact because the lab kits make instructional sense? Does the principal tell the science teacher that she must pay for the kits herself, that the district will not? Does the principal refuse the order and send the kits back to the company?

All of the solutions seem to me to have the potential to blow up in the face of the principal. Sending the kits back and forcing the teacher to reorder them using them using the proper procedures may delay the lesson for the students and cost the district more in terms of shipping and handling. Approving the PO after the fact will send a mixed signal to your staff if you have taken a firm stand on the issue of POs. Asking the teacher to pay for the kits herself is likely to be viewed as insulting. The answer is not clear, but the message is; welcome to the principalship.

I hesitate to give this as an example at the risk of offending coaches, but my experience demonstrates that the worst offenders for circumventing the purchase order process are the coaches. Few things are more frustrating than having fifty t-shirts show up to be used in a summer basketball camp and there is no purchase order. The coach is often the icon in the community and for the new principal to "buck" this person may be a recipe for disaster. Not to be overly officious, but it will come down to who is running the financial procedures of the building, the principal or the staff. Hopefully, you have communicated a warm and accessible personality, not to mention a collaborative attitude, from the first day on the job and have made clear your parameters for what you expect in regard to money matters. Expect cooperation from most of your staff.

I had been the superintendent in this particular district for three days when a parent came to me with a complaint against the cheerleading sponsor. The cheerleaders had recently had a 'corn boil' at the local celebration to raise money. This parent, who served as the president of the booster club, felt that the cheerleading sponsor had pocketed some of the money because there was not enough money left in the cheerleading account to send the girls to camp. There was no treasurer. The cheerleading sponsor served in that capacity.

The paper trail for how much corn was originally purchased and how much was sold was sketchy to non-existent. This was a classic case of "He said—She said." The situation was resolved, but had financial guidelines been in place this type of problem would not likely have arisen.

Issues concerning field trips that your teachers want to take are financial issues that tie directly to the curriculum. Because a field trip (unless the class is walking to a nearby location to the school) is going to cost the district some transportation dollars at least, the trip must be justified by linking the field trip to the curriculum. If the trip can not be connected to the curriculum then there is no reason for wasting the time of the children.

After the trip has been curricularly justified the teacher may collect a small amount of money from each student to help pay for the trip. This money collected is sent to the office immediately. Establish this procedure and the principal will set a tone of high expectations both for curricular instruction and for the proper handling of student money. Student money, or money of any nature, should not be left in the classroom.

A school district got into difficulty for collecting $30 from students for a class trip to be taken at the end of the school year that was to be a reward for good conduct. Prior to the day of the trip five students were notified that they did not qualify because of behavior problems during the year. They were not allowed to go on the trip. This seems straight-forward enough as the rules were clear to all. The issue that the parents raised with the principal was that the $30 was not going to be refunded to the students not allowed to participate.

The position of the principal was that plans were made for all of the students to participate and that the individual money collected from each student was an integral part of the total cost of the bus, admission to the amusement park, food, etc., to whatever was being planned. The issue went to the school board. There is no need to tell you what happened in this particular incidence, because absolutely any resolution is possible depending upon who the people and children are that are involved.

Vending services in your school can be a nice source of additional revenue for your building or just another unneeded headache for the principal depending upon how it has been setup and how the principal handles it.

The large soda companies will typically compete for the right to sell their product throughout the school district. The new principal upon arriving at her building may already find that Pepsi is the soda under contract. If this is the case, then Pepsi it will be until the contract expires. If Pepsi has established a full-service vending contract with the district then the vending company will oversee all aspects of the business. Your building will receive a periodic commission check. The principal should not have to worry about filling the machine, collecting the money, or the storage of the product. If the soda vending machine malfunctions, just call the company. The principal's time commitment is minimal.

There are other options besides full-service vending. Your building might operate its own vending business, purchase and store the product, fill the machines, and collect the money. The potential to realize a much larger profit is available with this method; however, it will involve more time and effort on the part of someone in your building. The potential for employee malfeasance is also increased.

Should you decide to place vending machines in your building think first about security for the stock of the product. Where under lock and key are you going to keep it? Who will have access? Someone will need to fill the machine and collect the money. What will happen when the machine is giving a two for one unadvertised special, or the machine is not dispensing any change or product at all? Who is going to make sure that the machine always has a supply of the necessary change?

Mutter and Parker[9] in their excellent financial guide discuss questions that the principal should ask the bookkeeper. The first week on the new job would be a wonderful time to ask these questions. After all, you need to meet this person anyway and asking questions like these suggest that you are savvy. If the bookkeeper indicates to you that problems exist, now is the time to correct them. Among the questions that I would deem crucial are:

1. Are the bank deposits being made daily by all groups? If not, how much is being kept in the building, and where is it being stored and secured?

2. Are there any sponsors or teachers who are not following purchase order procedures?

3. Are there any pending financial items we need to discuss?

4. Do you as the bookkeeper have any special bookkeeping concerns or suggestions for improvements?

Not only do you get to meet the bookkeeper with your questions, but this is an example of proactive communication at it's finest.

10

Final Things

There is more, oodles more, that a beginning principal will need to know about building financial procedures. Experience is going to be the best teacher, which comes only with, of course, experience.

The purpose of this book is to refresh and help direct the beginner, because if you are like me, you took your school finance class some time prior to your first principalship.

Becoming an astute budget planner and financial thinker means that you need to keep as up to date as possible on what is happening, particularly in your state. Belonging to your state's principals' organization is an excellent way of doing this.

There is a German word, *korinthenkacker*, which means that a person is overly concerned with trivial details to the point of letting important matters slide. Former President Carter was said to be so officious that he scheduled the use of the White House tennis courts himself. You would have thought that his time could have been better utilized.

As the principal you think that you will be responsible for everything that happens in your building, and to some extent this is true. However, remember that budget construction will comprise approximately only 3% of your time. You are communicating 100% of your time whether you know it or not. Communicate confidence.

How will you communicate financial matters to your stakeholders? From the very inception of your arrival, make certain that your school policies dealing with money matters are out front for all staff to see. Let it be known that your building will operate under sound bookkeeping and business procedures.

Purchase orders, the petty cash fund, change funds, and money that is handled by the teachers all have policy and procedures in place so that everyone knows what is expected. Make exceptions and deviate from your policies at your own risk.

Share with parent organizations that if the need is present you will arrange for someone to detail financial principles to help them keep the paper trail of money. This is not casting dispersions on anyone, but simply good business. Share this offer in person as you meet these groups for the first time and reiterate the offer annually.

It would be an excellent idea if every treasurer of school organizations was given in-service training prior to assuming the role.

Ask your building secretary if she feels comfortable with the financial responsibilities that she has. If not, provide in-service training.

As principal, require a monthly report from all of your school organizations, both parent and student activity, as to the financial transactions of the preceding month. This information can be compiled and dispensed in a monthly newsletter to all the stakeholders of your building, with a copy going to the superintendent and school board in your monthly report.

All of your building activity accounts should be made available to your stakeholders every month in the form of a newsletter. The superintendent and board of education will require this information anyway so it will be readily available for you to disseminate.

It is likely that most of your stakeholders will not care particularly if you begin the year with $500 budgeted for art supplies and as of February $480 of that that original amount had been spent. Whether they are interested or not in this particular item is not really the point. The point is that you make all of your buildings financial dealings available for public consideration.

This type of information brings 'sunshine' to financial matters and gives everyone the impression that there is nothing to hide and will help your site-based committee make better financial decisions about the next year's budget. Provide the financial stuff before you are asked.

At some point in the fall once you have settled into the role of principal, you should go over the district budget with your staff, particularly where your own building is concerned. As you recall from your days as a teacher, most of your staff will not have a clue how to interpret the various expenditure funds, functions, and objects. By assisting them they will be able to find in the district's budget just exactly how much money you are receiving in compensation.

I would suggest that you consider periodically meeting with department heads, the local union, or whoever the key players on your staff are. Go over the financial picture in as much detail as necessary, asking for input and suggestions on matters that are within the control of the building.

Good morale is something that all principals want and sometimes principals communicate that desire by providing staff with items that have a dollar and cent cost attached to them. Token gifts given to staff should be generated by staff dollars or donated by some organization such as the PTA. Some districts will allocate district dollars for incentive or recognition gifts to staff that come from the general fund. I would make sure that these gifts are useful in the classroom. Presenting your entire staff with sweatshirts that have your school mission statement on them with tax generated dollars may sound like a wonderful idea, but could the money have been better spent on the education of the kids?

Why should the taxpayers contribute to a gold watch at the time of retirement, or even a plaque that recognizes outstanding contributions to the district for the past thirty years? Sure, it is a nice gesture and a wonderful photo opportunity, but you need to find money that is not tax payer generated. Maybe the principal or superintendent should go door-to-door and ask for donations for the gold watch. That might prove to be an enlightening experience.

I once had a school board member who in her first meeting as a newly elected representative proposed what she thought was a wonderful idea to honor and recognize excellence in teaching and extra effort. She proposed that the principal at each of the schools would select one staff member each quarter at their school who was demonstrating extra effort. This extra effort could include extra time spent outside of the classroom or a certain teaching or activity in the classroom that enhanced learning. The nominee might also be a non-certified staff member that was delivering extra effort.

After selecting this one individual, the principal would write a short paragraph or two outlining the staff member's reason for the nomination. The principal forwards the nomination to the superintendent, who in turn provides the board of education the anonymous reviews for consideration. The board votes on the nominees and determines a winner each quarter. No one was to know who the nominees were, except for the principal.

The individual selected each quarter would receive a gift certificate of $25 to the café or his choice in the community; a commendation in his personnel file; a certificate from the board of education; and his photo accepting the awards from a school representative.

The board member outlined in her proposal the following benefits for all concerned:

For the school—1) added employee morale; 2) allows district to reward those who contribute extra effort; and 3) portrays the school in a positive light by showing off the accomplishment of staff.

For the staff member—1) recognition from everyone for a "job well done;" and 2) a $25 gift certificate for dinner.

For the cafes in town—1) someone actually goes there to eat. (This is not part of the proposal and is intended as a 'funny' on my part.)

Although this may have been a noble contribution on the part of the new board member, the idea was not well received by staff. The teachers' union did not trust the principals to make meaningful evaluations and they questioned the competitive nature of the plan because all staff contends that they are giving "extra effort." To the dismay of the new disheartened board member, the teachers insisted that this idea would horribly damage morale. Furthermore, the board member was stunned when teachers asked where the money would come from to provide for the free dinner and certificates?

The board member looked to me for the answer to that question. Never being able to provide a truly straight answer, I responded "The money tree out back." This answer is not recommended, unless you clarify it by saying that this money tree grows in the property taxes that are collected throughout the district.

There is no money tree, of course. There are only citizens to be coddled and convinced that their dollars are needed to provide quality education to the children of the community.

The inequitable financing of public education seems to defy a political solution. It is a concern of mine, but I will never solve the problem. It should be a concern of yours too, and I hope you will solve the problem. Education is a state issue, as the U.S. Constitution is silent concerning education; therefore, the 10th Amendment is applied.

The U.S. Supreme Court case that stopped school finance cases in the federal courts was *San Antonio v. Rodriguez* in 1973. *Rodriguez* was determined by a 5-4 decision that stated that wealth is not a suspect classification because of the disparity created by the wide gap caused by poor and rich school districts in per-pupil spending. The U.S. Supreme Court declared that education is not a fundamental right. Getting a good education in this country is like having a fine meal or driving an expensive automobile. You can have access to only what you can afford.

Fixing the school funding inequities is not up to the U.S. Supreme Court or Congress, but is left to the legislators of the various states. My position is that state politicos are not going to find an equitable solution enabling all children to receive the type of education that the richest school districts provide.

Perhaps the federal government should become a more involved player in financing public education. Currently, federal dollars average about 8% of the total money invested in education in the country.

There seem to be federal dollars available to 'fix' other social problems. Senator John McCain states in his recent book that "the cost to the federal government for covering insured deposits lost by the failed thrifts (savings & loans), if apportioned to every American citizen, would eventually approach $2,000 for every man, woman and child."[10] Wouldn't it have been wonderful if poor school districts had received an extra $2,000 for every citizen in the district?

There is a perfectly good word that is seldom used today that was more prosaic prior to the American Civil War. *Spitchcock* is the word and to be spitchcocked as a principal will not be a pleasant experience. It means to handle roughly and severely, perhaps even to eviscerate and cook on a spike.

I saw a new principal trying to explain an upcoming tax referendum to the Rotary Club one afternoon and the principal was indeed spitchcocked by a group of very knowledgeable citizens. It was embarrassing and the principal should never have been placed in a position of trying to explain something that he did not thoroughly understand.

Pick your communicative battles carefully.

Despite the best efforts to find and correct every calculation and error in this book, some will still exist. Rest assured that they remain in place on purpose, to ensure that you read carefully.

I leave you with this quote from the old television series '*Leave It To Beaver.*' It applies to this book and education, and life as well.

Beaver: Gee, there's something wrong with just about everything; isn't there Dad?
Ward: Just about Beav.

I welcome your comments at: charles.waggoner@enmu.edu

NOTES

1. *USA Today,* January 6, 2005. "Hungry Black Hole Emits Mighty Burp". Page 10D.

2. *Education Week,* March 9, 2005. "Audit Says N.Y. District Lost $11.2 Million to Theft Spree." Page 4.

3. *Launching Your First Principalship: A Guide For Beginning Principals.* Barbara L. Brock and Marilyn L. Grady. Corwin Press: Thousand Oaks, California. 2004.

4. http://www.iasaedu.org/sampleresolution.pfd

5. *Freakonomics: A Rogue Economist Explores The Hidden Side of Everything.* Steven D. Levitt and Stephen J. Dubner. William Morrow publishers. 2005. Page 165.

6. http:www.geocities.com/schoolfunding/equity_in_education_project.htlm

7. http://www.boston.com/news/education/k_12/articles/2005/06

8. *Financing Education in a Climate of Change.* Vern Brimley, Jr. and Rulon R. Garfield. Pearson Publishers, 9th edition. 2005. Page 324.

9. *School Money Matters.* David W. Mutter and Pam J. Parker. Alexandria, Virginia: Association for Supervision and Curriculum Development. 2004. Page 124.

10. *Worth The Fighting For.* John McCain. New York: Random House. 2002. Page 167.

THE MATRIX REVIEW

MATRIX # 1—*If you cannot be ethical and honest please do not assume the leadership position of principal in the school.*

MATRIX # 2—*If you don't know the answer—find someone who does.*

MATRIX # 3—*Do not assume anything as a principal when you are communicating financial matters of the building or district. Thoroughly explain your terms; not everyone in your audience has a working understanding.*

MATRIX # 4—*It takes money to run the schools and the money will come from only a limited number of sources. No matter the source, you will only be able to utilize the dollar amounts that are available in the budget.*

MATRIX # 5—*If you can't explain something that affects you directly (such as your own tax bill) then the assumption is likely to be that you have some gaps in your understanding of how the district is funded.*

MATRIX # 6—*Politicians have one goal and that is to be re-elected to office.*

MATRIX # 7—*As a principal, sometimes you just have to settle for "close enough" and let it go.*

MATRIX # 8—*The best predictor of the future is the past. Find out all you can about what has gone before.*

MATRIX # 9—*Educating your publics concerning financial matters is a constant and on-going process.*

MATRIX # 10—*A good principal will avoid running out of money in his building at almost any cost.*

MATRIX # 11—*If you cannot find what you are looking for in your office, just figure that your disgruntled predecessor trashed it or stole it, and go ask for a new one.*

MATRIX # 12—Have a contingency plan always and in financial matters have a 'contingency account fund.'

MATRIX # 13—Do not knowingly place your superintendent on a financial hot spot.

MATRIX # 14—As with most considerations, give those with issues that impact finance your undivided attention; promise to consider the issue; consider the issue in the manner it deserves; and get back as soon as possible with your response.

MATRIX # 15—No matter how powerfully you contemplate the budget, there is still a lot of guesswork involved in the final product.

There were fifteen matrixes mentioned in the book, however, there is a final one that I will share with you. As I informed you, I like lines from movies, finding that many are applicable to education.

One such line is from a John Wayne movie, I think it may be *Big Jake*, where John Wayne turns to someone and says, "Don't pee down my back and tell me it's raining."

Like Wayne's character, the principal will be the recipient of all kinds of advice, both well intended and the misdirected. With experience comes the wisdom of knowing which advice is rain and which is pee. Both may feel warm at the time, but only one is truly refreshing.

BONUS MATRIX—With experience will come the ability to ferret out what works and what doesn't.

At no point in this book has any religious scripture been quoted. It is now time. The last sentence of Acts 26:14, as reported in the *King James Bible*, states that: "It is hard for thee to kick against the pricks."

Other translations of the Bible will substitute the word 'goads' for pricks. No matter what your particular translation says, I believe the statement to be true.

There is a saying among New Mexicans that if you walk into the wild here everything will sting you, bite you, or prick you. In other words, regard every living thing as a potential source of danger.

As a principal you will be goaded or pricked by people, many that you had perceived to be your supporter. Loyalty shifts like the sands and the problem for the principal will be to determine just where the pricks in any given situation are coming from. This is a complicated and difficult undertaking and although experience will help you in this matter, be prepared to be surprised from time-to-time.

HELPFUL WEB ADDRESSES

http://nces.ed.gov
    National Center for Educational Statistics

http://www.bea.doc.gov/bea/regional/gsp/
    Bureau of Economic Analysis

http://www.npbea.org
    National Policy Board for Education Administration

http://www.acess.gov.gov
    U.S. Government Printing Office

http://www.ed.gov/index.jhtml
    U.S. Department of Education

http://www.doe.state.in.us/htmis/states.html
    Department of Education for all states

http://raw.rutgers.edu/raw/gasb
    Governmental Accounting Standards Board

http://nces.ed.gov/pubs2004/2004318pdf
    Financial Accounting for Local and State School Systems

978-0-595-36393-3
0-595-36393-8

Printed in the United States
95484LV00004B/377/A

9 780595 363933